SAILING
THE BASICS

SAILING
—THE BASICS—

DAVE FRANZEL

INTERNATIONAL MARINE PUBLISHING COMPANY
Camden, Maine 04843

©1985 by David Franzel

Typeset by The Key Word, Inc., Belchertown, Massachusetts
Printed and bound by The Maple/Vail Book Manufacturing Group, Binghamton, New York

Published by International Marine Publishing Company
21 Elm Street, Camden, Maine 04843
(207) 236-4342

Library of Congress Cataloging in Publication Data

Franzel, David.
   Sailing: the basics.

   Bibliography: p. 129.
   Includes index.
   1. Sailing. 2. Seamanship. I. Title.
GV811.5.F73 1985   797.1'24   85-2513
ISBN 0-87742-201-X

CONTENTS

PREFACE

Years ago I had a student at the Boston Sailing Center who, after completing a "Learn to Sail" course and sailing on his own several times, returned from a particularly glorious sail one day and proclaimed for all who cared to listen: "Sailing is like life, only more so!"

Of course, this guy was only a beginner. But like life, sailing can take you in many directions—from messing about in a little boat on a lake, to windsurfing, to daysailing, to local cruising, to coastal cruising, to ocean cruising, to dinghy and one-design racing, to handicap racing, to ocean racing, and more. And when you consider that within any one of these realms you will experience a wide range of wind, wave, and numerous other conditions, as well as the pleasure of understanding a bit more about sailing each time you go out, this beginner was not that far off.

Whichever direction sailing may take you, however, it is generally best to start at the beginning, which brings me to the purpose of this book. As the text for the "Learn to Sail" course at Boston Sailing Center, this book is designed to guide a newcomer through all the information necessary to sail safely and well. Since sailing safely and well requires a thorough knowledge of the basics, my goal for this book is to develop in readers an appreciation for why things work the way they do as opposed to restating traditional litanies that pass for understanding.

For example, ask 100 sailors how a sail generates force to drive a boat against the wind, and 95 of them will tell you about "Bernoulli's Principle" and leave it at that. Notwithstanding Mr. Bernoulli's excellent credentials, his principle provides little visual or intuitive explanation of what actually occurs as wind flows over sails or how that translates into moving a boat.

This book endeavors to offer points of view that may be readily visualized. In my experience teaching sailing, I have found that the more thorough one's understanding of the underlying reasons why things work, the more readily one moves on to more advanced concepts. This process, in my opinion, makes learning more fun. And the more fun one has while learning, the better one learns, and the more exciting it becomes to learn more. And so on.

This book was written with the importance of thorough understanding as a guiding principle. Therefore, where possible, new concepts are derived from or follow from previously discussed information. One purpose in presenting information in this manner is to make it easier to read and to avoid the problem many sailing texts have of presenting new information without connecting it to what has gone before. Another purpose is that this developmental approach corresponds to one of the ways by which I hope readers will continue to refine their knowledge of sailing after they finish the book.

A few beginners have told me that they feel the sections on balance and sail shape are unnecessarily taxing for individuals not interested in racing. I could not disagree with this more. Sailing with your boat balanced, heeling no more than necessary, and above all maintaining control at all times are every bit as important to cruising or daysailing as they are to racing. A knowledge of proper sail-shape control is essential to sailing safely under a wide range of wind and wave conditions regardless of the type of boat you sail. On the other hand, there is a lot of new information in those sections, and I recommend that you not expect to digest it all in one reading, but rather read it and then refer to it as you continue sailing until the information becomes clear.

This book is intended as a thorough presentation of the basics. It is not intended to be the last word on any subject contained herein. I've included a bibliography for further information on specific subjects. On the other hand, no book or individual has all the answers on any subject. Experienced sailors continue to learn more every time they sail. The more experience you gain, the finer the points you learn. That's the beauty of sailing. Enjoy!

TYPES OF SAILBOATS

There is a wide variety of boats you can sail; each type of boat creates its own sailing experience. A view of the different categories of modern sailboats will help you see what you are getting into.

CENTERBOARD OR KEEL?

One of the main attributes that differentiates a sailboat from other craft is the underwater blade that helps keep a sailboat going straight and prevents it from slipping sideways, even against a powerful sideways wind. There are two types of blades that serve this purpose: keels and centerboards.

A keel is a fixed structure securely attached to the underside of the hull. It invariably weighs a lot (typically 40 to 60 percent of the boat's total weight), which makes a keelboat very stable (Figure 1.1).

A centerboard, on the other hand, is a blade that can pivot from a straight-down position up to a fully retracted position inside the boat. This is desirable when there is no sideways wind or when you want to land on a beach.

While centerboard boats enjoy several advantages over keelboats (price, speed, and sensitivity, for example), they do capsize more easily. However, while accidental capsizing can be extremely unpleasant and in some cases dangerous, many of the modern, relatively small centerboard boats designed with large, watertight flotation tanks (the Laser, 420, 470, Flying Scott, Lark, and Sunfish, to name but a few) are relatively easy to right again and generally come up dry and ready to sail (Figure 1.2). You can usually right a centerboard boat by standing on the centerboard (Figure

Keelboats, on the other hand, are virtually impossible to capsize. As a keelboat heels over in progressively stronger wind, two things happen. The amount of sail area exposed to the wind decreases, and the force of gravity acting on the keel tends increasingly to right the boat. A keelboat is therefore self-righting (Figure 1.3).

Both centerboarders and keelboats have a variety of sailing uses. Small centerboard boats (8 to 15 feet), while quite responsive and sensitive to what you do

Figure 1.1   The Soling

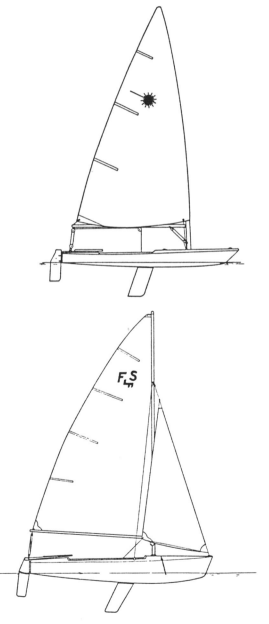

Figure 1.2   *Three popular center-board classes: Right, The Laser; Lower left, The 470; Lower right, The Flying Scot*

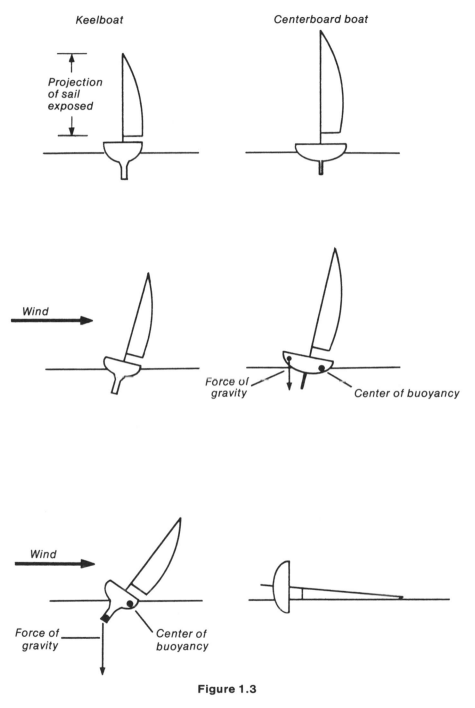

Figure 1.3

The weight of the keel prevents a keelboat from ever heeling much more than this.

A centerboard boat will tend to stay like this until you right it by standing on the centerboard.

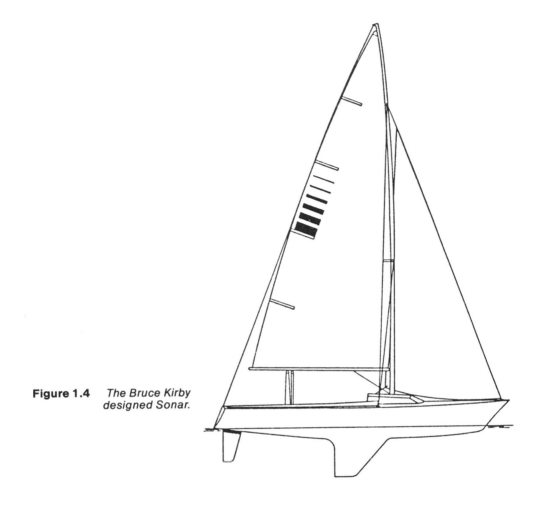

Figure 1.4 *The Bruce Kirby designed Sonar.*

with your weight, are relatively tame in light to medium wind conditions, which makes them good learning boats for kids and other agile people.

Some of the larger centerboard classes are extremely fast and challenging under good conditions and make use of the most modern sailboat technology, and these qualities make many centerboard classes popular for racing.

By contrast, keelboats, which with a few exceptions begin at about 18 feet, are especially well suited to family daysailing or coastal cruising. Even some of the smaller keelboats have large cockpits and easily handled rigs. The Sonar (Figure 1.4), for example, is stable and fast; has a spacious, comfortable cockpit; and is a superb, "one-design" racing boat as well.

Accommodations suitable for coastal cruising—cabin, berths, galley, head, icebox, etc.—can be found in keelboats about 24 feet in length and up. A seaworthy keelboat between 24 feet and maybe 34 feet might be a good choice for a first cruising boat. You can cruise the coast of Maine during the summer and within a year or two learn enough to sail down the East Coast to the Bahamas in autumn. Cruising at sea in a sailboat you trust is one of the most enjoyable things you can do (Figure 1.5).

Figure 1.5 *A typical cruising sloop.*

But like centerboarders, some keelboats are also excellent boats on which to learn to sail. At the Boston Sailing Center, for example, we use 27-foot Olympic class Solings. These boats have a fin keel (deep and short) and a spade rudder (a good distance behind the keel) that gives tremendous turning leverage. The Soling is as maneuverable as most centerboard dinghies; at the same time, its keel weighs 1,300 pounds, which, at 60 percent of the total weight of the boat, makes the Soling virtually impossible to capsize. All these characteristics make the Soling one of the best boats for sailing instruction (Figure 1.6).

DIFFERENT RIGS

Sailboats may also be classified according to type of rig. By this system, a given sailboat may be a sloop, catboat, cutter, ketch, yawl, or schooner.

Sloops like the Soling have one mast, a mainsail, and a jib. On some sloops you

Figure 1.6

Aft is that way ← | Forward is that way →

Transom

Rudderpost | Topsides

Spade rudder

Fin keel

Hull

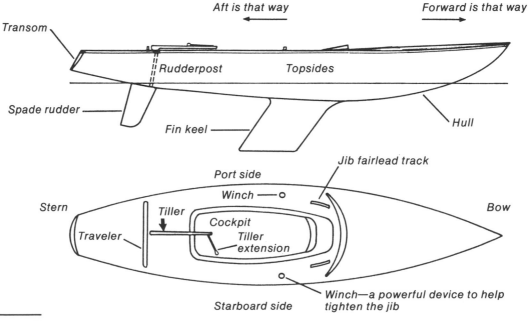

Jib fairlead track

Port side

Winch ──o

Stern

Tiller

Cockpit

Bow

Traveler

Tiller extension

Winch—a powerful device to help tighten the jib

Starboard side

Figure 1.7 *Catalina 30 showing a genoa.*

have the option of carrying either a jib or a *genoa*, which is just a large jib (Figure 1.7).

A boat that has one mast and only one sail is called a *catboat* (Figure 1.8). On a catboat, the mast is stepped much farther forward than on a sloop. The reason it would not do simply to take the jib off a sloop and call it a catboat is this: balance.

If you sail a sloop with just the mainsail, the wind force acts too close to the stern. This tends to blow the stern downwind, pivoting the bow around towards the wind— a nasty situation when you want to go straight. (Note: This does not imply that a sloop won't sail on just the main; only that it will not sail *well* on just the main.

To avoid this, the catboat's mast is farther forward than on a sloop so that the sail force is distributed evenly fore and aft. *Fore* means toward the bow; *aft* means towards the stern.

A one-masted boat with the mast located farther aft than on a sloop will generally have two headsails (jibs). Such a rig is known as a *cutter*. (The precise definition of a cutter is a one-masted boat on which the mast is located at least 40 percent of the way aft as measured at the waterline.) (Figure 1.9.) A cutter rig gives you more power up front without the necessity of a large and sometimes unwieldy genoa.

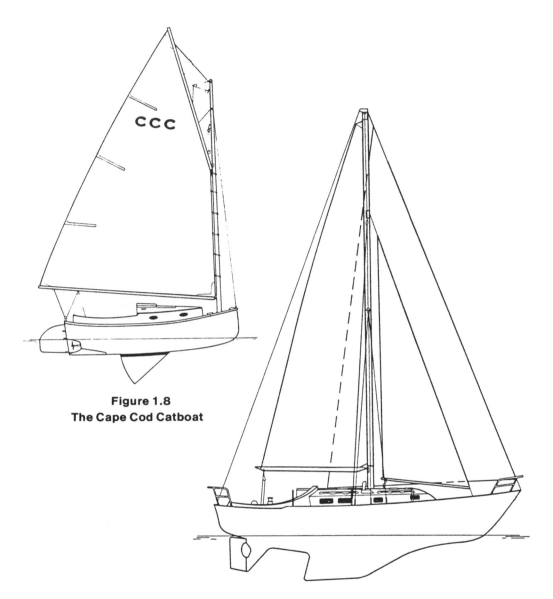

**Figure 1.8
The Cape Cod Catboat**

Figure 1.9   Cutter, the Southern Cross 35

In rigs with two masts of different sizes, the taller mainmast may be forward or aft. If the mainmast is forward, then the boat is either a *ketch* or a *yawl*, and the shorter after mast is called the *mizzen*.

On a yawl, the mizzen is a tiny little thing positioned aft of the rudderpost and the helmsman and is therefore out of the way (Figure 1.10). On a ketch (Figure 1.11), the mizzen is located forward of the rudderpost and therefore can be larger and more effective. On traditional ketches, this leaves the helmsman behind the mizzenmast, which may obscure his vision in some cases. Because of this fact, some modern

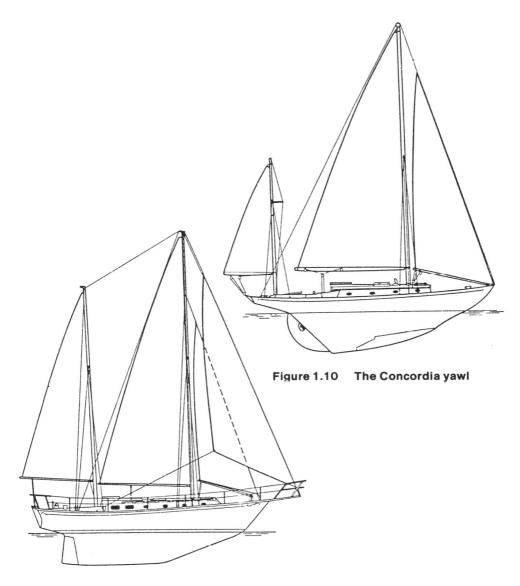

Figure 1.10   The Concordia yawl

Figure 1.11   Ketch, an aft cockpit Shannon 38

ketches have the steering wheel rigged forward of the mizzenmast in a *midships cockpit* configuration, although the rudderpost itself is aft of the mizzenmast and the rig is still, properly, a ketch (Figure 1.12).

If the mainmast is aft, then the boat is a *schooner*, from the 18th-century expression, "see how she schoons" (Figure 1.13). The forward mast is called the *foremast*. Schooners, while not famous for their ability to sail against the wind, are quite fast in other directions and are among the most beautiful boats anywhere.

Any of these *split rigs* (i.e., yawls, ketches, and schooners) have their sail areas

Figure 1.12
The Irwin 41, a midships cockpit ketch

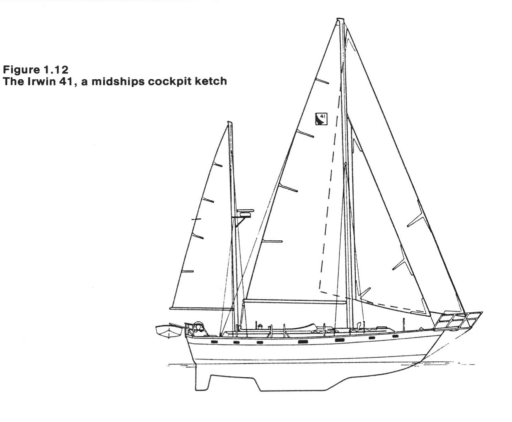

Figure 1.13
Schooner, the Worldcruiser 44

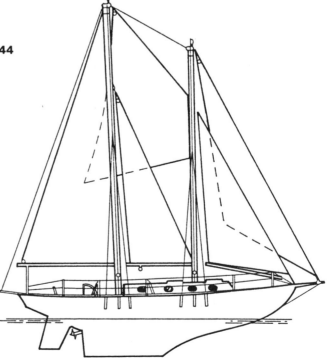

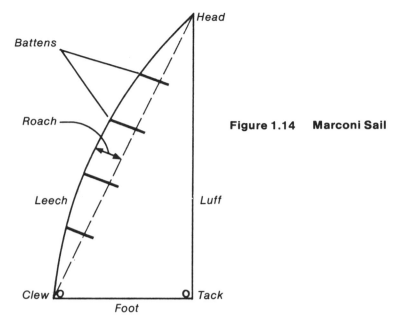

Figure 1.14   Marconi Sail

spread out and therefore do not require as tall a mainmast as would a comparably sized sloop to achieve the same total sail area. The result is that the main and genoa are somewhat smaller and therefore easier to handle on a split rig.

Solings and most other modern boats have a triangular or *marconi* mainsail. This is by far the most efficient sail for sailing against the wind (which, as it turns out, you spend much of your time doing) because it most closely corresponds to the shape of a wing. Indeed, a marconi sail functions just like a wing when sailing upwind, as you will see.

It is called marconi because the modern mast and rigging required to handle the forces that such a sail develops resemble a radio tower, the radio having been invented around the turn of the century by Marchese Guglielmo Marconi. Those who think this does not entitle Marconi to so much credit call the triangular main a *Bermuda* sail.

Marconi or Bermuda, the triangular sail has three corners and three edges, the names of which—*tack, clew, head, luff, foot,* and *leech*—you should know (Figure 1.14). The *roach* is the area between the leech and a straight line drawn from the head to the clew. *Battens* are slats of wood or fiberglass inserted in pockets sewn in the sail that prevent the roach from flapping.

RIGGING

The rigging of a boat is divided into the *standing rigging*, which supports the mast and the *running rigging*, which controls the sails.

Standing rigging consists of *shrouds*, which support the mast sideways and *stays*, which support the mast fore and aft. On most boats the stays and shrouds are "tuned" once or twice per season by means of *turnbuckles*, which tighten or loosen them.

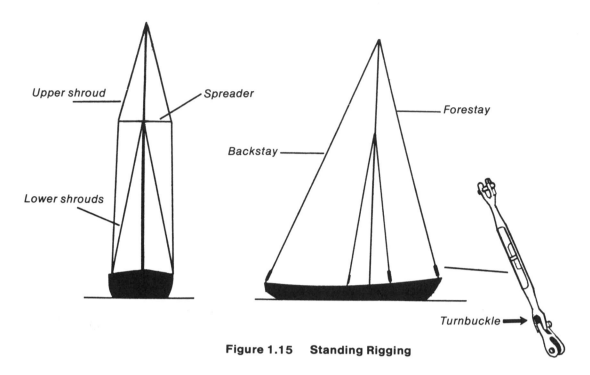

Figure 1.15   Standing Rigging

Spreaders spread the upper shrouds so they make a more effective angle for supporting the top of the mast (Figure 1.15).

Running rigging consists mainly of *halyards*, which raise and lower the sails and *sheets*, which ease the sails out and trim them in. On a Soling and one some other boats, the halyards are internal; that is, they run inside the hollow mast.

Other parts of the Soling's running rigging are the *outhaul, downhaul, cunningham,* and *boomvang* (Figure 1.16).

BENDING ON THE SAILS

"Bending on the sails" (attaching them to the boat and preparing them to be raised) is a fairly straightforward process best learned by doing it a couple of times. However, a brief description of the steps involved and a couple of suggestions related to general seamanship (the art of staying out of trouble) might help.

One of the most important things to keep in mind from the moment you get ready to board a boat, whether from a slip or from another boat, is to *keep all parts of your anatomy out from between your boat and anything else.*

Place your sailbags directly into the cockpit—not on the deck—so that you won't be embarrassed by your sails falling off the boat (most sails don't float). If the boat is a relatively small centerboard boat, you should step into the center of the cockpit to avoid tipping the boat. If the boat is a stable keelboat, you can step onto the deck, but remember the warning in the previous paragraph.

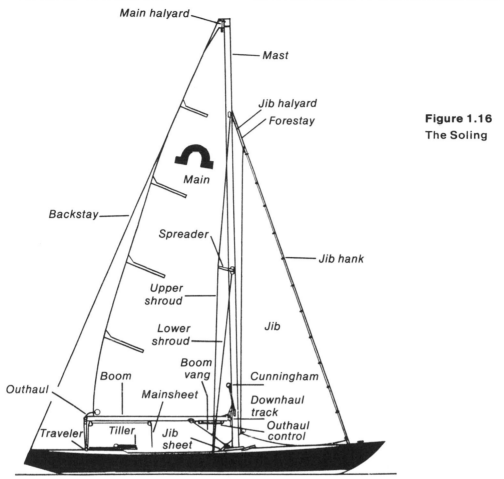

Figure 1.16
The Soling

To rig the mainsail, first find the clew of the sail and, clew first, feed the foot *boltrope* into the groove in the boom. Attach the tack *cringle* (grommet or hole) to the appropriate fitting on the *gooseneck* (the place where the boom joins the mast), then attach the *outhaul* to the clew cringle and tighten it. Run your hands along the luff from the tack to the head to ensure that it is not twisted, then attach the main halyard to the head of the sail and feed the luff rope into the groove in the mast. As you do this, pull the other end of the halyard and secure it so the first couple of feet of luff rope stay in the mast groove. Insert the battens into their pockets.

To rig the jib, begin by attaching the tack of the sail to the appropriate fitting at the base of the forestay (or the *jib downhaul*, if your boat has such a thing), then work your way up the luff of the sail, attaching the *hanks* or *snaps* to the forestay one at a time. Keep the sail low as you do this, particularly if it is windy. *Reeve* the *jib sheets* through the *fairlead blocks* (thread them through their respective pulleys) and tie *stopper knots* in the ends of the sheets so they cannot pull out of the fairlead blocks. Loosen the jib halyard and shackle it to the head of the sail. Your sails are now ready to be raised. Don't raise them yet, though—we have to talk about sailing first.

2

WIND AND POINTS OF SAIL

efore hoisting sail and setting out on your first voyage, it's important that you understand the interaction of wind and sail, resulting in your boat's forward movement—or lack thereof.

HOW WIND ACTS ON SAILS

Let's assume the wind is northwest (this means "blowing from the northwest") and you want to sail your boat towards the southeast.

Clearly, you will sail most efficiently if you present the greatest projection of sail area to the wind. You do this by setting the sail at a right angle to the boat on either the port or the starboard side (Figure 2.1).

Now suppose that you want to sail across (at a right angle to) the wind (Figure 2.2). You can do this with the wind coming over your starboard side or with the wind on your port side.

It is not difficult to see how a boat develops power sailing across the wind. Consider:

1. The keel or centerboard is a blade that essentially keeps the boat in a track, prevents it from slipping sideways, and only lets it move forward.

2. If you throw a rubber ball against a wall (Figure 2.3), it bounces off at the same angle at which it hits, and the force at the point of impact is exactly perpendicular to the wall.

So when a wind molecule hits a sail, it bounces off and generates force perpendicular to the sail (Figure 2.4). This force has a lateral component that is cancelled out by the keel or centerboard (except for some heeling, or leaning, of the boat) and a forward component, or *driving force*, that makes the boat go forward (Figure 2.5).

At this point, we should take time out to talk about the wind.

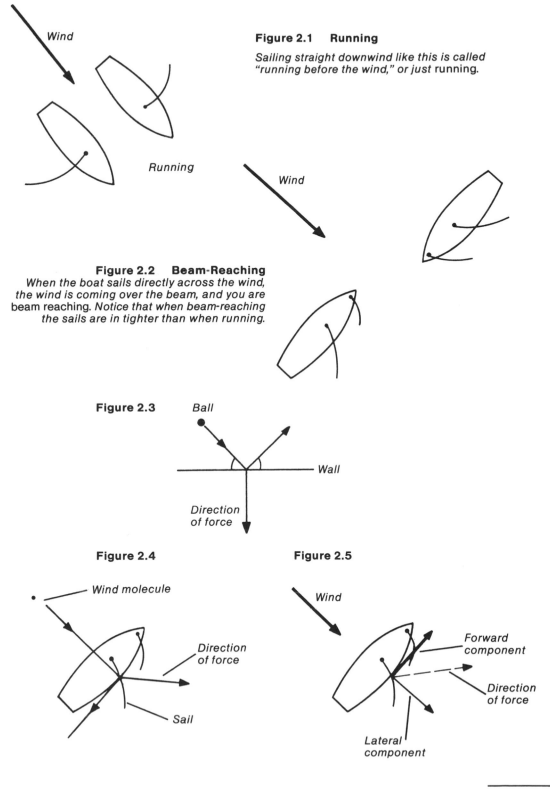

Figure 2.1   Running

Sailing straight downwind like this is called "running before the wind," or just running.

Wind

Running

Wind

Figure 2.2   Beam-Reaching

When the boat sails directly across the wind, the wind is coming over the beam, and you are beam reaching. Notice that when beam-reaching the sails are in tighter than when running.

Figure 2.3

Ball

Wall

Direction of force

Figure 2.4

Wind molecule

Direction of force

Sail

Figure 2.5

Wind

Forward component

Direction of force

Lateral component

WIND DETERMINANTS

The little arrows that we're using to represent wind direction are much easier to see on paper than they are in real life. Therefore, since you don't have such handy clues to wind direction when you're on the water, sailing depends upon keeping track of the wind direction. It is wise to become familiar with some of the visible indicators of wind directions called wind determinants:

1. *Telltales*, pieces of yarn tied to the shrouds.
2. Cigar or cigarette smoke on board.
3. Moored boats. They usually point into the wind.
4. The smallest waves. They roll downwind. (The larger waves often tell you what the wind was doing yesterday.)
5. Birds. They usually sit on the water facing into the wind so they don't ruffle their feathers.
6. Your geographical orientation. If you know the wind is blowing from up the harbor, for example, you can determine the wind direction at any time simply by looking up the harbor.

   Any of these techniques work, and there are others too. The point is to be able to relate the wind direction to the boat at any time so you know whether you are on a run, a beam reach, or any of the other three *points of sail*, and whether the wind is coming over the port or the starboard side.

PORT TACK AND STARBOARD TACK

Any object in the wind has a *windward* side (side towards the wind) and a *leeward* side (downwind side).
   A boat underway is either on a *port tack* or a *starboard tack*, corresponding to that side of the boat is windward (Figure 2.6). The mainsail will naturally tend to blow to the leeward (pronounced *looard*) side of the boat. Because of this, *leeward* is defined as the side the mainsail is on and *windward* as the other side. The mainsail of the first

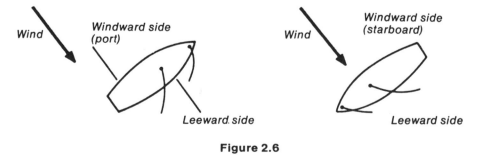

Figure 2.6

*This boat is beam-reaching
on a* port tack.

*This boat is beam-reaching
on a* starboard tack.

boat in Figure 2.7 is on the starboard side; therefore, starboard is leeward, port is windward, and the boat is on a port tack. The second boat is on a starboard tack.

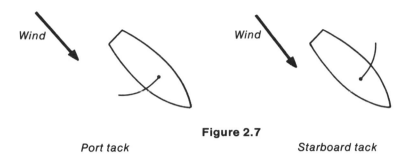

Figure 2.7

Port tack   *Starboard tack*

STEERING

A boat steers by means of a rudder, which on small boats is attached to a tiller. The rudder works like this (Figure 2.8): If the boat is moving forward through the water, then the water is moving backwards with respect to the boat. Consider the effect this will have on the rudder (and hence on the stern of the boat to which it is attached) if you put the helm (tiller) to port. If you move your tiller to the left, the boat turns right.

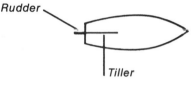

Figure 2.8

If you move your tiller to the right,the boat turns left (Figure 2.9). Notice, however, that for this to work as described, the boat must be moving forward.

If you're not moving (as when you first leave your mooring, for example), or if you're moving backwards (yes, this sometimes happens), then you cannot steer in the conventional manner described above. Fortunately, there are ways to steer when you're not moving forward, and we will get to them later.

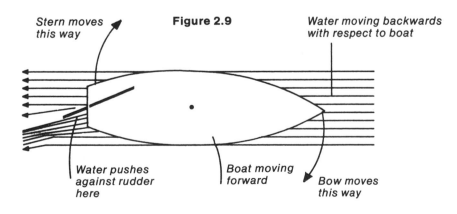

Stern moves this way   **Figure 2.9**   *Water moving backwards with respect to boat*

Water pushes against rudder here   *Boat moving forward*   *Bow moves this way*

SAILING UPWIND

Now if you're sailing on a beam reach and gently move the tiller to the leeward (leeward is the side the mainsail is on), the boat will "head up" towards the wind. If, as the boat heads up, you haul the sheets (the lines that control the sails) in tight, you find that you maintain drive and keep sailing well, as close to the wind as 40 to 45 degrees on either tack in most modern boats (Figure 2.10). If you try to head up closer to the wind when you're close-hauled, the sails will begin to *luff* (flutter), and you will lose drive.

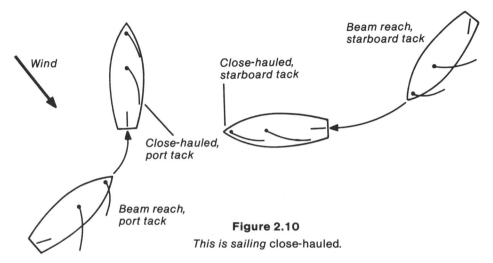

Figure 2.10
This is sailing close-hauled.

Close-hauled means sailing as close to the wind as possible.

It is somewhat incredible that a modern boat can sail fast, as close to the wind as 40 to 45 degrees. There are two factors that enable a boat to do this:

1. The keel or centerboard, which resists the lateral component of the wind force and only lets the boat go straight.

2. The fact that sails are not flat—they are curved like wings and work exactly like wings in generating the force that drives the boat. Observe what happens to the air flow as it encounters the sail (Figure 2.11): It gets split by the luff into air that flows along the windward side of the sail and air that flows along the leeward side. The air on both sides, however, then changes direction to flow along the surface of the sail towards the leech. It is easy to see how the air on the windward side of the sail is

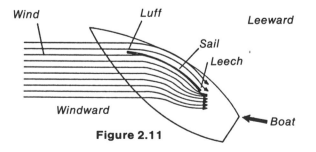

Figure 2.11

forced to alter its direction aft, but why should the air on the leeward side of the sail do the same? The answer lies in a principle called *attached flow* (Figure 2.12).

Air likes to flow in a straight line. If the sail were not there, the air would keep going straight. As soon as the air begins to flow across the leeward side of the sail, however, the surface of the sail begins to curve away from the straight path that the air would like to travel. The instant the air tries to travel its straight path, it begins to diverge from the curved surface of the sail. Of course, if the air leaves the surface of the sail, then there is no air at the surface of the sail. No air means a relative vacuum, and this relative vacuum holds the air flow close to the sail. This occurs at every point

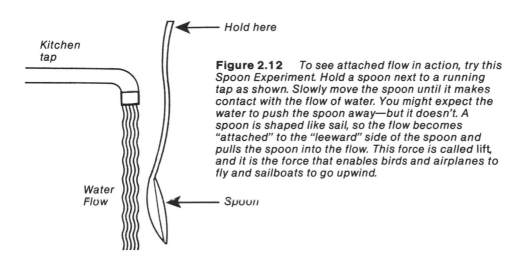

Figure 2.12 *To see attached flow in action, try this Spoon Experiment. Hold a spoon next to a running tap as shown. Slowly move the spoon until it makes contact with the flow of water. You might expect the water to push the spoon away—but it doesn't. A spoon is shaped like sail, so the flow becomes "attached" to the "leeward" side of the spoon and pulls the spoon into the flow. This force is called lift, and it is the force that enables birds and airplanes to fly and sailboats to go upwind.*

as the flow continues over the leeward side of the sail because the sail curves continuously from luff to leech.

So in effect, the air flow becomes "attached" to the leeward side of the sail and changes direction to flow parallel to the curve of the sail.

Now clearly, force is required to alter the course of the wind stream, and the same force that pulls the wind stream towards the sail at every point also pulls the sail towards the wind stream at every point. This force is called *lift*, and it acts at right angles to the sail at every point (Figure 2.13). The change in direction of the air flow on the windward side also contributes to this force. The total force acting on the sail in

Figure 2.13

Lift acting at right angles to a sail at every point. It turns out that most of the force is generated in the front part of the sail, which is fortunate because the front part of the sail generates force more in the direction you want to go.

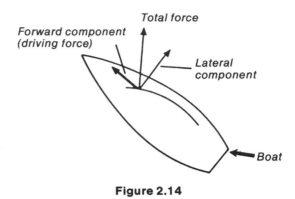

Figure 2.14

Figure 2.14 may be viewed in terms of its forward component and its lateral component. The forward component drives the boat ahead; the lateral component does not push the boat sideways (because of the keel or centerboard) but rather may cause the boat to heel.

Now that we know something about sailing close to the wind, let's see about sailing to an upwind destination.

Since you can sail as close to the wind as 45 degrees on either tack, there is a 90-degree section that you cannot sail directly into (see Figure 2.15). Yet much of the time, as it turns out, the wind is coming from where you want to go. In order to get to a destination located upwind, you must sail close-hauled, *close-hauled* is as close to the wind as you can sail, first on one tack, then the other, zigzagging your way upwind.

Figure 2.15

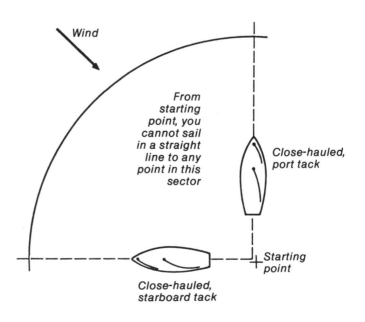

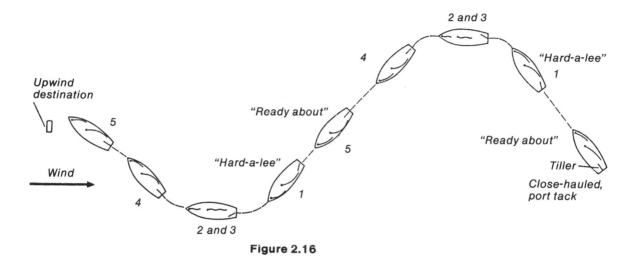

Figure 2.16

TACKING OR COMING ABOUT

Changing from one tack to the other when heading upwind is called *tacking* or *coming about*. It works like this (Figure 2.16):

1. Helmsman puts tiller to the lee side (towards the mainsail). Boat begins to turn into the wind.
2. At this point, boat is directly into the wind and the sails luff completely. Boat keeps turning.
3. Crew has released old jib sheet . . .
4. . . . and trims new one in as helmsman straightens the course of the boat.
5. When sails fill on the new tack, helmsman straightens the course of the boat. Boat is now close-hauled on a new tack.
6. You have arrived at your upwind destination.

From the point of view of people in the boat, two things happen during a tack. First, the boom swings across the boat—do you know why it's called boom?—and second, the jib, which is controlled only by its leeward sheet, must have its old leeward sheet released and the new one trimmed. Therefore, it is a good idea for the helmsman to warn his crew when he is going to tack. The traditional commands are "Ready about" (which means "get ready") and "Hard-a-lee" (which means "here goes, I'm pushing the tiller to the lee side now!).

BEATING

Working your way upwind, coming about a number of times, and sailing close-hauled on either tack in between is called *beating*.

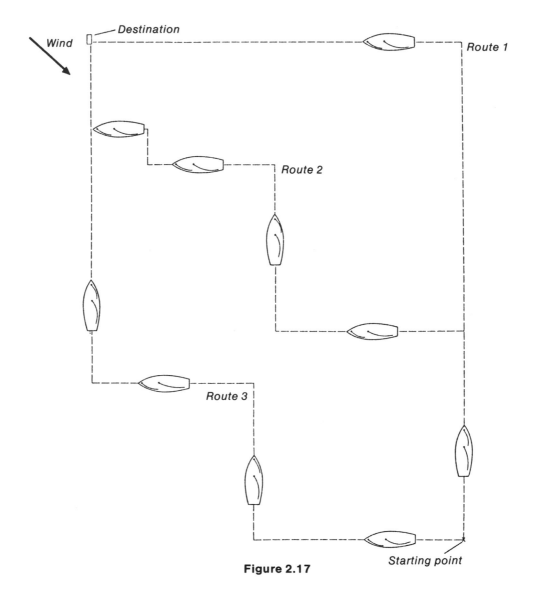

Figure 2.17

Notice that there are an infinite variety of routes you can take to get to an upwind destination. You can come about once or many times (Figure 2.17).

The word *tack* can be a bit confusing since it has three different meanings:

1. It may refer to the lower corner of a sail.
2. It may refer to the windward side of the boat, as in the expressions "port tack" or "starboard tack."
3. It may refer to coming about.
4. It is often used incorrectly to mean beating, taking a series of tacks to get upwind.

Notice also that if the wind is steady, the distance traveled using any of the possible routes is the same (add the verticals and the horizontals of each route). However, during the time it takes you to tack, there is no force driving the boat; thus, you lose speed each time you tack. If the wind is perfectly steady, you get upwind faster using fewer tacks. But the wind is rarely perfectly steady, and later we will discuss how you can use small shifts in wind direction to get upwind even faster than you can when the wind is steady.

JIBING

There are two ways to change from a port to a starboard tack or *vice versa*. One way is tacking. When you tack, the boat turns upwind, the bow crosses the wind, and the sails fill on the new tack.

The other way is *jibing*. When you jibe, the boat turns downwind towards a run and then keeps turning past the run so the stern of the boat and the leech of the mainsail cross the wind.

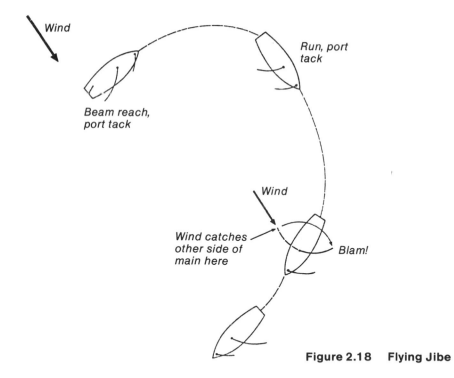

Figure 2.18   Flying Jibe

Suppose the fellow who is beam-reaching in Figure 2.18 *falls off* (turns to leeward—leeward is the side the mainsail is on) toward a run, easing out his sails as he does so. If he then keeps turning, there comes a point when the leech of the mainsail crosses the wind, which then catches and fills the other side of the main and blows it across the boat—rapidly!

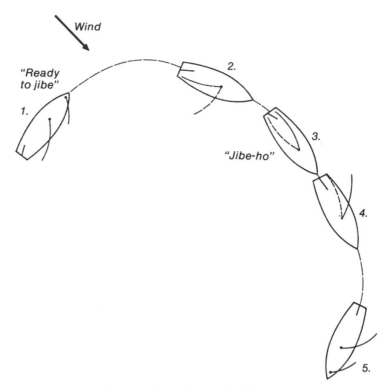

Figure 2.19   Controlled Jibe

This type of jibe is called a *flying jibe* or an *accidental jibe,* and it can be hard on the head, not to mention the equipment. To avoid the shock of having the boom swing rapidly across the boat when jibing, you must do a *controlled jibe.*

To do a controlled jibe, haul in on the mainsheet as the boat approaches a run so that by the time the boat comes onto a run, the sail is in about as tight as possible. This prevents the boom from accelerating across the cockpit. After the main leech crosses the wind, you immediately ease the main sheet out again, thus absorbing the shock of jibing even in a very strong wind.

In other words, here are the steps involved in a controlled jibe (Figure 2.19):

1. Bear off to leeward towards a run.
2. As you approach a run, steering carefully, haul in the mainsheet until the boom is nearly in the center of the boat.
3. Keep turning; if the main is nearly centered, you don't have to turn far before the leech of the main crosses the wind and you jibe.
4. Immediately after the main jibes, ease it right out on the new tack.
5. Straighten up on your desired course.

The key to doing a controlled jibe properly is to recognize with certainty when the boat is approaching a run and when you are about to jibe. One way to do this is to

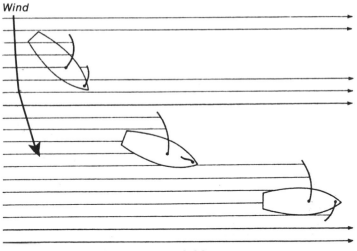

Figure 2.20

keep an eye on the telltales, which indicate wind direction. Another way is by feel. As the boat approaches a run, even in strong wind, it stops heeling as the lateral force subsides.

But perhaps your best source of information is the jib. You may have noticed by now that the jib has so far been excluded from pictures that show a boat running. This is because, as the boat approaches a run, the mainsail blocks the wind from filling the jib. Suddenly, the jib loses its wind and tries to wander over to the other side (Figure 2.20).

"Why, then," the alert student asks at this point, "bother with jibing since it seems quite difficult, not to mention dangerous?" Here's why: To sail from "here" to "there" it may be necessary to sail around buoys that mark shoals. And with practice, jibing is neither difficult nor dangerous (Figure 2.21).

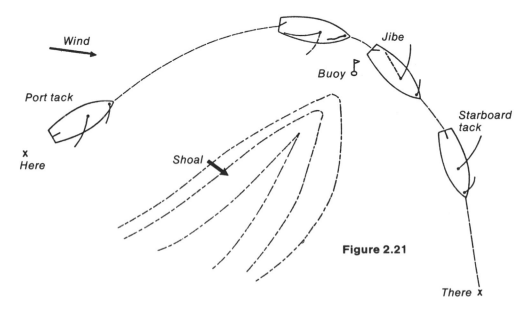

Figure 2.21

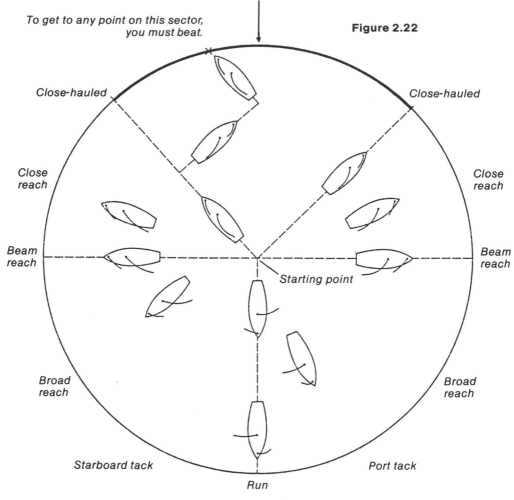

To get to any point on this sector, you must beat.

Figure 2.22

Close-hauled   Close-hauled

Close reach   Close reach

Beam reach   Beam reach

Starting point

Broad reach   Broad reach

Starboard tack   Port tack

Run

POINTS OF SAIL

By now you have probably realized that words like *close-hauled*, *beam reach*, and *run* each refer to a course of the boat relative to the wind.

- *Close-hauled*, a boat sails as close as possible to the direction the wind is coming from.
- *Beam-reaching*, a boat sails at a right angle to the wind.
- *Running*, a boat sails straight downwind.

These three are called *points of sail*. There are two others:

- *Close-reaching*, when a boat sails closer to the wind than on a beam reach but not as close as when close-hauled.
- *Broad-reaching*, when a boat sails farther downwind than when on a beam reach but not as far downwind as on a run.

These five points of sailing describe all possible angles between the boat and the wind.

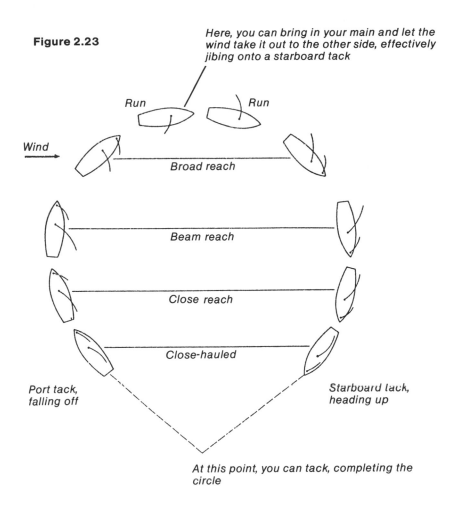

Figure 2.23

Here, you can bring in your main and let the wind take it out to the other side, effectively jibing onto a starboard tack

Run

Run

Wind

Broad reach

Beam reach

Close reach

Close-hauled

Port tack, falling off

Starboard tack, heading up

At this point, you can tack, completing the circle

Notice also that when close-hauled you trim your sails in quite tight; when beam-reaching you set them about halfway out; and when running you ease them out all the way.

It should therefore come as no surprise that when close-reaching you set your sails in tighter than when beam-reaching; and when broad-reaching you ease your sails out farther than when beam-reaching.

Figure 2.22 outlines the five points of sail and the approximate sail trim for each. For each of these trips from the starting point to a point on the circle, think about the angle between the boat and the wind. The five points of sail name these possible angles and to a large extent describe what the sailing is like.

Let's consider a boat sailing in a circle (Figure 2.23). As it does so, it passes through each point of sail. Turning to leeward—the side the mainsail is on—is *falling off*. Turning to windward is *heading up*. As you fall off, you ease out your sails. As you head up, you trim in your sails.

The previous two diagrams give a rough picture of how sails are set for each point of sail, but let's examine the criteria for setting your sails exactly right on any point of sail. First, though, we should review what we know about how sails work.

SAIL TRIM

We have described two types of force that drive a boat. When you're sailing close-hauled, air flows along the surface of the sails, and lift drives the boat. When you're sailing downwind, the sails are *stalled*—there is no air flow along the surface of the sails—and the boat is powered by wind driving into the sails and pushing the boat.

On reaches, the boat is powered by a combination of lift and pushing. The closer the reach, the more lift; the broader the reach, the more pushing.

Of the two types of force, lift is more powerful. Whenever possible, we want to get air flowing along the leeward side of the sails. Therefore, on any point of sail except very broad reaching or running, we try to set the sails to achieve the most effective airfoil possible. We also try to get the direction of force (which is always at right angles to the sail) to point as far forward as possible (so we go forward rather than heel). This means we want the sails as far out as they can be as long as they do not luff (flutter on the leading edge). This is the key to perfect sail trim.

A good rule of thumb is: If a sail is not luffing, ease it out. If it is luffing, trim it in until it stops. Trim both your main and jib in this manner (Figure 2.24). This technique, easing the sails out until they luff a bit and trimming them in just until the luffing stops, works on any reach.

When close-hauled, you always want to sail as close to the wind as possible, so it is up to the helmsman to maintain perfect trim through steering. Here's who to do it:

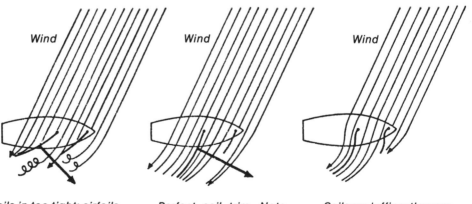

Sails in too tight; airfoils stalled; direction of force is more sideways than it should be.

Perfect sail trim. Note that direction of force points more forward.

Sails are luffing; they are out too far and should be trimmed in just until they stop luffing.

Figure 2.24

With sails trimmed in tight, gently head up closer to the wind. When you head up too close, the jib begins to luff and the boat "stands up" and slows down. As soon as you notice this, fall off again just until the jib stops luffing. This is a perfect close-hauled course. When sailing close-hauled (which you will spend a good deal of time doing), you are constantly "testing" your course by heading up until you see the jib luff and then falling off until it stops luffing. Keeping the boat in the groove like this when beating is an art. You must test your course constantly without deviating from the perfect close-hauled course (Figure 2.25).

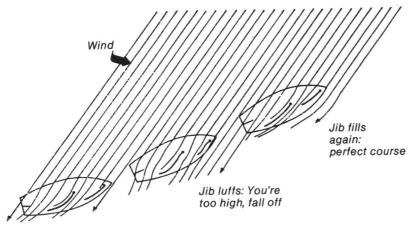

When close-hauled, to be sure that you are really as close to the wind as you can sail, gently head up until you see the jib luff, then fall off just until the jib stops luffing.

Figure 2.25

When running, your mainsail should be all the way out. The jib will not function on the leeward side since there it would be in the wind shadow of the main. For the jib to be of any value when running, you should take it over to the windward side. Sailing like this is called sailing *wing-and-wing*, or *wung out* (see Figure 2.26).

If your destination happens to be straight downwind and the wind is not too shifty, you will probably run wing-and-wing to get there.

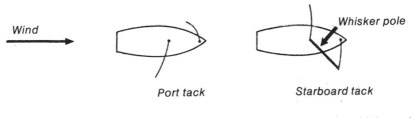

You can usually rig a whisker pole to hold the jib to windward more effectively.

Figure 2.26   Running wing-and-wing

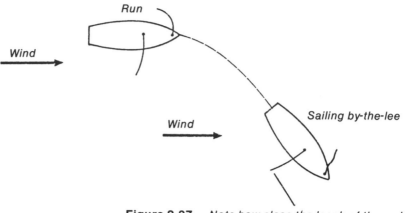

Figure 2.27 *Note how close the leech of the main on this boat is to crossing the wind. This would result in an accidental jibe.*

If the wind is shifty or if it is one of those nice, easy-going days, you may forget to steer carefully, accidentally turn to leeward, and put yourself in danger of an accidental jibe.

If, mistakenly, you have turned to leeward when on a run but have not yet jibed, you are sailing *by-the-lee*. Sailing by-the-lee is so called because the wind is then coming over the leeward side of the boat (Figure 2.27). It is dangerous to sail by-the-lee because you are then extremely close to jibing accidentally.

If you see that you are by-the-lee, you can avoid an accidental jibe by pushing the tiller to leeward, toward the mainsail.

Whether or not you're likely to be sailing by-the-lee or jibing accidentally, if the wind is shifty it can be a hassle to steer wing-and-wing so that the jib stays full without continuously filling explosively. Therefore, if your destination happens to be downwind and conditions are difficult, it may be easier to broad-reach on one tack, do a controlled jibe, broad-reach on the other tack, etc., to get to your downwind destination. This procedure is called *tacking downwind*. In fact, you sail faster on a broad reach than you do on a run, so the extra speed may compensate for the extra distance you travel when tacking downwind (Figure 2.28).

The information on points of sail and sail trim applies for all sailboats whether they are keelboats or centerboard boats. However, with a centerboard boat there is an additional element to be considered, and that is the position of the centerboard on each of the five points of sail. In general, the farther down you have your board, the more effectively it resists the lateral component of force generated by the wind. When you're sailing close-hauled, with maximum lateral force to resist, your board should be all the way down. When you're running, with negligible lateral force, you can raise your board all the way, reducing water friction and increasing speed (usually by a substantial amount). In fact, as you fall off progressively from a close-hauled course

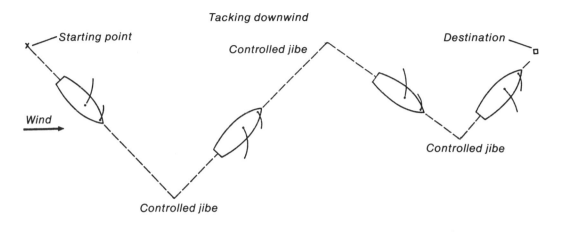

Figure 2.28

and ease out your sails, the lateral component of force steadily subsides, and you can gradually raise your board.

Of course, there are exceptions to this. Sailing downwind in respectable waves, a boat tends to roll (oscillate from side to side). This is particularly likely if your board is all the way up. In fact, running in waves with your board up can lead to the dreaded "death roll," wherein each roll takes you a bit farther than the last until you capsize. Of course, when you capsize with your centerboard fully retracted, righting the boat becomes quite challenging, since the board is no longer readily available to stand on! When running in waves, therefore, keep the centerboard down somewhat to minimize rolling.

See page 52 in the chapter on balance and sail shape for another exception to these guidelines on centerboard position.

3

GETTING STARTED

ow that we have covered some of the basics of sailing, we can discuss taking off from a mooring.

LEAVING A MOORING

Secured at a mooring, your boat will usually point into the wind. This makes sense if you consider that the boat is moored from the bow and so the rest of the boat will tend to be blown downwind. It will point elsewhere only if the wind is shifting so fast that the boat can't figure out where it's coming from or if the boat is affected by a strong current from a different direction.

In any case, it is best to get both sails rigged and ready to be raised before you raise either one. (You may wish to review the procedure for bending on the sails outlined at the end of Chapter 1.)

If the boat is pointing generally into the wind, it is best to raise the mainsail first, for two reasons: First, the main is aft, and if it fills the stern will tend to be blown downwind, keeping the boat pointed nicely into the wind. This gives you time to cleat and coil your halyards, etc. Second, luffing wildy in the wind is one of the worst things that can happen to a sail, especially to a jib (the weight of the boom prevents the main from being damaged quite as readily). Permitted to luff wildly, the jib will not only flog itself to shreds but will cause some of the strangest knots to occur in the jib sheets.

Prior to hoisting the main halyard, be certain that the downhaul or cunningham, boom vang, and mainsheet are released so the boom will be able to go up and swing freely as the sail is raised. Keep an eye on the battens and be sure that they don't get hung up on the edge of the cockpit or between a lower shroud and the mast, for example. Once the sail is *all the way up* (look aloft to be certain), secure the halyard and tighten the cunningham or downhaul and the vang.

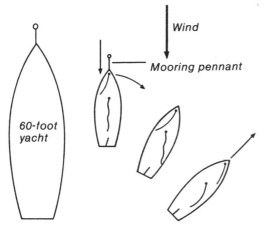

Figure 3.1

If you grab the clew of the jib and hold it out to port, it will fill on its port side. Since the jib is on the bow, this will push the bow to star-board.

Once you have got the boat turning the way you want, you can release the mooring. The boat will then respond as shown here.

Before hoisting the jib, be sure the sheets are free. Raise the sail, secure the halyard, and if your boat has a jib downhaul, tighten it to get some tension on the luff of the sail.

Once the sails are up, it is best to get underway as quickly as possible. But suppose: There you are at your mooring, sails raised, and there is a 60-foot yacht moored nearby on your port side, with the owner aboard! Clearly, you want to turn to starboard, and you don't want any possibility of error. Remember that when you first cast off your mooring pennant you are not moving, and when you are not moving you cannot steer by means of the tiller.

One technique for steering when you are into the wind and not moving is called *backing the jib* (Figure 3.1). Backing the jib, by the way, is also an excellent technique for getting out of *irons*, which is what you get into when you make the mistake of heading into the wind long enough to lose speed and steerageway. When in irons you cannot steer with the tiller but you can back the jib.

Just as important as understanding how backing the jib works is realizing that invariably the wind shifts and the boat oscillates on its mooring so that it frequently does not point directly into the wind (see Figures 3.2a and 3.2b). If, when you are

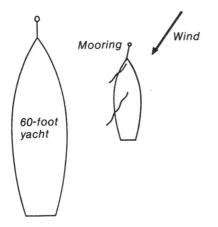

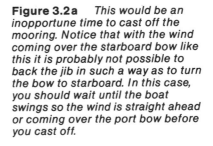

Figure 3.2a *This would be an inopportune time to cast off the mooring. Notice that with the wind coming over the starboard bow like this it is probably not possible to back the jib in such a way as to turn the bow to starboard. In this case, you should wait until the boat swings so the wind is straight ahead or coming over the port bow before you cast off.*

Figure 3.2b *An alternative tactic that might speed things up in this case would be to hold the main to starboard. Since the main is closer to the stern, this would push the stern to port, turning the bow to starboard.*

As the boat then turns back into the wind, back the jib to port as soon as doing so will cause it to fill and turn the bow to starboard. At that moment you can cast off the mooring.

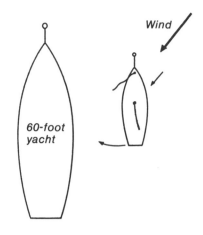

ready to raise your sails, the boat is not headed into the wind, it may be difficult to raise the mainsail, as the battens will tend to catch under the shrouds and the boat will begin to sail while it is attached to the mooring and you are struggling with the main, all of which can make for an embarrassing situation. Much better in this case would be to raise the jib first, sail out under jib alone into clear water, head up into the wind, and then raise the main.

If the boat is at a dock instead of a mooring, you might secure the bow to a dock cleat so that the boat points into the wind and swings freely as if it were at a mooring. Then you can raise the main, then raise and back the jib to choose your direction.

Sometimes the wind is too shifty for this, or it is blowing onto the docks. Then the best solution might be to paddle out into open water, head into the wind, raise the main, get underway, and then raise the jib. If your boat is equipped with an auxiliary engine, it is generally safest to leave the dock under power, motor into open water, head into the wind, raise your sails, and then shut off your motor.

LEEWAY

Up to now, we have referred to the keel or centerboard as if it were a magic blade that only permits the boat to go in a straight line. Well, this is not exactly the case (Figure 3.3). Even the most sophisticated racing boats with the most up-to-date keel shapes will slip a few degrees to leeward when sailing upwind.

To understand about leeway, let us look more closely at how a keel works. Imagine a clear glass boat moving through the water (Figure 3.4). Bear in mind that water will flow by the boat exactly from the direction in which the boat tracks. Observe as the water flows past the keel. You can imagine that the faster you go, the stronger the lifting effect of the keel and the closer you sail to a straight course. The faster you go, the less you slip; the slower you go, the more you slip.

So when you first leave your mooring and pull in your sails, you will find that you move sideways until you begin to pick up forward speed. This is an important fact to

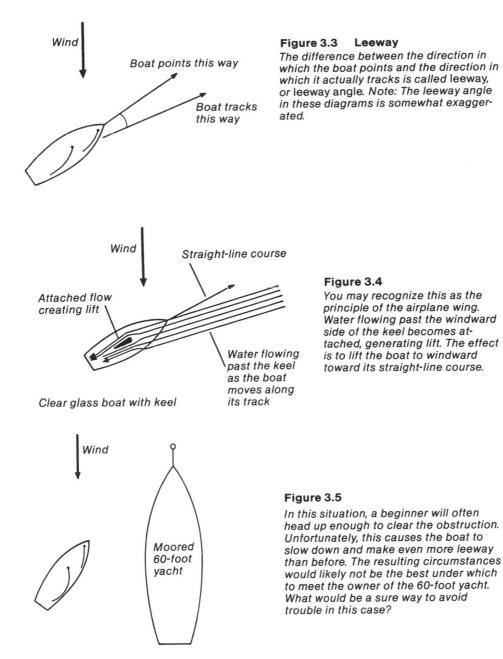

Figure 3.3   Leeway
The difference between the direction in which the boat points and the direction in which it actually tracks is called leeway, *or* leeway angle. *Note: The leeway angle in these diagrams is somewhat exaggerated.*

Wind

Boat points this way

Boat tracks this way

Wind

Straight-line course

Attached flow creating lift

Water flowing past the keel as the boat moves along its track

Clear glass boat with keel

Figure 3.4
You may recognize this as the principle of the airplane wing. Water flowing past the windward side of the keel becomes attached, generating lift. The effect is to lift the boat to windward toward its straight-line course.

Wind

Moored 60-foot yacht

Figure 3.5
In this situation, a beginner will often head up enough to clear the obstruction. Unfortunately, this causes the boat to slow down and make even more leeway than before. The resulting circumstances would likely not be the best under which to meet the owner of the 60-foot yacht. What would be a sure way to avoid trouble in this case?

keep in mind whenever you are sailing in the vicinity of rocks, piers, shoals, other people's boats, etc.

In fact, there is a kind of silly problem that beginning sailors often get into that is so common that it merits mentioning here. And that is this: trying to *pinch* (sail too close to the wind) to clear an obstruction to leeward (Figure 3.5).

TRUE AND APPARENT WIND

Suppose you go out to your sailboat and there happens to be no wind, zero knots (a *knot* is one *nautical mile* per hour, or about 1⅙ land miles per hour). Undaunted, you decide to take out a paddle and start stroking, and before long you get the boat moving forward at three knots. What do you feel? Tired? Ridiculous? Yes, but although the true wind is zero knots, you feel a wind of three knots coming from straight ahead, a wind you are creating as a result of your speed. The fact is, any time you move forward, your motion creates a headwind.

When you sail, the effect is still there, the headwind created by your forward motion modifies both the speed and direction of the wind you (and the sails and the telltales) experience on the moving boat.

True wind is the wind you feel when you are not moving.

Apparent wind is the wind you feel on the moving boat. It is the true wind altered in speed and direction as a result of the forward motion of the boat.

There are some interesting manifestations of the difference between true and apparent wind, so let's look more closely at how they differ. Apparent wind is what you actually feel on the boat. When running, you are going with the wind, so the wind you feel—apparent wind—is actually less than the true wind. For instance, running at five knots in a 12-knot breeze, you feel only a seven-knot wind behind you (see Figure 3.6).

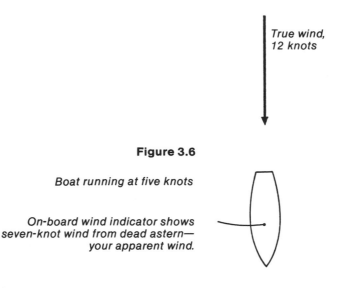

True wind, 12 knots

Figure 3.6

Boat running at five knots

On-board wind indicator shows seven-knot wind from dead astern— your apparent wind.

On a dead run, the speed of the wind is changed, but not the direction. On any point of sail other than a dead run, however, the direction of the apparent wind as well as the speed are altered by the forward motion of the boat. Specifically, *the wind is always shifted forward by the forward motion of the boat*. The faster the boat goes, the farther forward the apparent wind is shifted. Here's an example:

If you have ever had the pleasure of driving a convertible in the rain with the top down, you know that if you drive faster than about 35 miles per hour you don't get wet because the "apparent rain" comes from forward as a result of your speed. The people in the back seat, however, do get wet. If you drive above 60 miles per hour, you can keep the people in the back seat dry too, since the apparent rain then comes from even farther forward as a result of your greater speed. It's a lot of fun until you have to stop for a light, at which time the apparent rain is the same as the true rain, and everybody gets wet. Apparent wind works exactly the same way. When beating, you sail into the true wind, so the wind you feel on the boat is stronger than the true wind. If you could sail at five knots directly into the 12-knot true wind, the wind you would experience, your apparent wind, would be 17 knots. You can't, of course, so your apparent wind speed is really about 16 knots. Also, the apparent wind is always forward of the true wind, and if you are beating at 45 degrees to the true wind (as most boats do), you are actually sailing at 32 degrees to the apparent wind (see Figure 3.7).

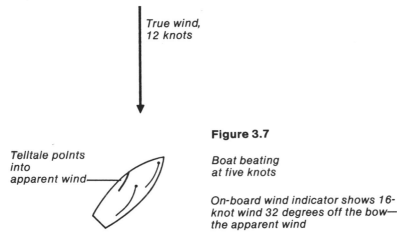

True wind, 12 knots

Figure 3.7

Telltale points into apparent wind

Boat beating at five knots

On-board wind indicator shows 16-knot wind 32 degrees off the bow— the apparent wind

Notice that in the same 12-knot wind you feel 16 knots beating and only seven knots running.

So one important ramification of the difference between true and apparent wind is that you may leave on a downwind course, warm and happy, wind at seven knots, but when you turn around to beat back, the wind is suddenly 16 knots and it's cold and waves are breaking over the bow and you wish you had brought a wool sweater and a windbreaker.

Here is another way the difference between true and apparent wind makes itself known. Consider sailing at a right angle to the true wind. A beam reach? Nope. As always, the headwind created by the boat's speed shifts the wind forward, so the apparent wind—your wind—comes from forward of the beam. You are actually on a close reach; your telltale indicates that you are on a close reach, and you set your sails for a close reach (Figure 3.8).

In fact, to get onto the point of sail that you know as a beam reach, you have to fall off some to this position (see Figure 3.9). On this point of sail, the apparent wind—your wind—is at a right angle to the boat, and you are on a beam reach.

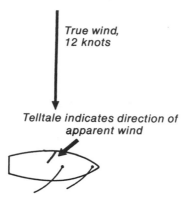

True wind,
12 knots

Telltale indicates direction of
apparent wind

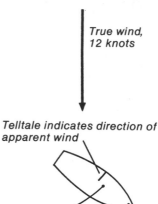

True wind,
12 knots

Telltale indicates direction of
apparent wind

Figure 3.8   *Boat sailing at a right
angle to the true wind, five knots*

Figure 3.9   *Boat sailing at a right
angle to the apparent wind—a beam
reach, but only 50 degrees or so from
a dead run*

Notice that from a beam reach, it is not a 90-degree turn to a run, as you might have thought, but substantially less. If your jibes have been sneaking up on you, this may be the reason why (see Figure 3.10).

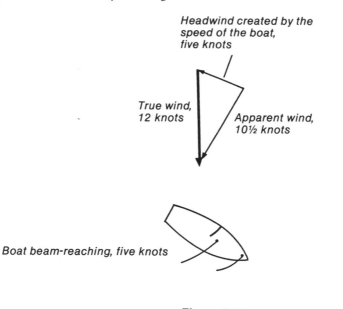

Headwind created by the
speed of the boat,
five knots

True wind,
12 knots

Apparent wind,
10½ knots

Boat beam-reaching, five knots

Figure 3.10

Now go back to the list of wind indicators in Chapter 2, page 16. Which of these techniques tell you the *true* wind direction?

MOORING

Often one of the most disconcerting things to a beginning sailor is the realization that "This goddarn boat's got no brakes." A sailboat can be stopped exactly where you want it to stop, however, and coasting into a perfect landing at your mooring, the boat stopping just as the bow touches the buoy, is a graceful and satisfying skill to master. It is also an important skill to master—especially to the owners of boats moored near yours.

To stop a boat, you must head up close enough to the wind so that when you free your sheets your sails luff *completely*. There will be no drive, and the boat will coast to a stop. To stop at a mooring, therefore, you must consider the wind direction and start luffing and slowing at some point downwind of the mooring to give yourself the distance you need to stop. It is important to be essentially stopped when you have a crew member reach for the mooring buoy. Otherwise, your crew member must decide whether to stay with the boat or the mooring.

There are two basic techniques for landing a boat under sail at a mooring. One good method is outlined in Figure 3.11: Locate a point a few boat lengths downwind

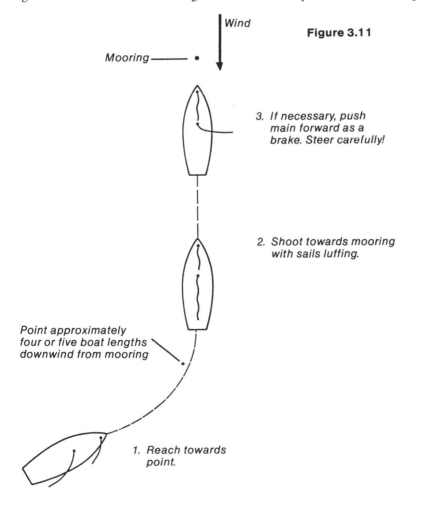

Wind

Figure 3.11

Mooring

3. If necessary, push main forward as a brake. Steer carefully!

2. Shoot towards mooring with sails luffing.

Point approximately four or five boat lengths downwind from mooring

1. Reach towards point.

from the mooring where you want to land. Estimating the exact distance needed to stop takes practice. A keel boat coasts farther than a centerboarder, *and in a strong wind you slow faster and so need less distance.* If you see that you will be moving too fast when you reach the mooring, you can push the mainboom forward and the sail will fill from its forward side and act like a brake.

A second technique, which provides a bit more control and which some find easier, involves approaching a mooring not exactly head-to-wind but on a close-hauled course with sails luffing (Figure 3.12). This gives you the advantage of being able to trim your main and gain speed if necessary—a thing you cannot do if you approach head-to-wind.

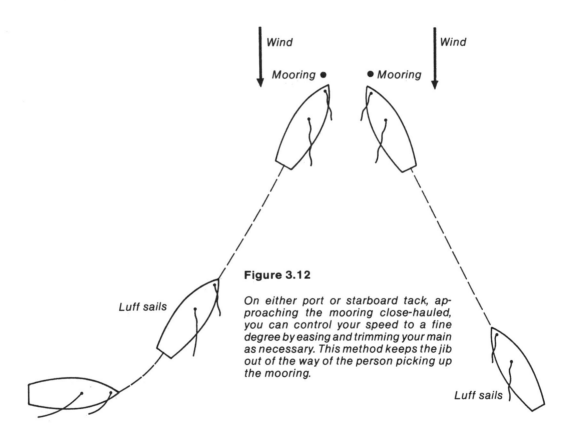

Figure 3.12

On either port or starboard tack, approaching the mooring close-hauled, you can control your speed to a fine degree by easing and trimming your main as necessary. This method keeps the jib out of the way of the person picking up the mooring.

Either of these techniques works well for landing at a mooring or for picking up a man overboard. It is important for the boat to be completely stopped—sails completely luffing—to accomplish either of these goals.

You can use these same techniques to land at a dock, provided the wind is blowing off the docks and is steady enough so that you can be sure it will not shift and blow you into the docks (Figure 3.13).

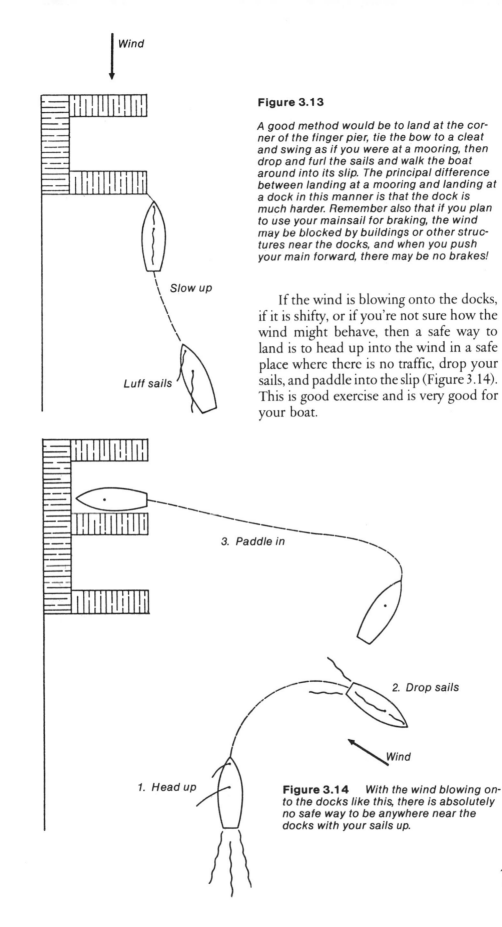

Wind

Slow up

Luff sails

Figure 3.13

A good method would be to land at the corner of the finger pier, tie the bow to a cleat and swing as if you were at a mooring, then drop and furl the sails and walk the boat around into its slip. The principal difference between landing at a mooring and landing at a dock in this manner is that the dock is much harder. Remember also that if you plan to use your mainsail for braking, the wind may be blocked by buildings or other structures near the docks, and when you push your main forward, there may be no brakes!

If the wind is blowing onto the docks, if it is shifty, or if you're not sure how the wind might behave, then a safe way to land is to head up into the wind in a safe place where there is no traffic, drop your sails, and paddle into the slip (Figure 3.14). This is good exercise and is very good for your boat.

3. Paddle in

2. Drop sails

Wind

1. Head up

Figure 3.14 *With the wind blowing on-to the docks like this, there is absolutely no safe way to be anywhere near the docks with your sails up.*

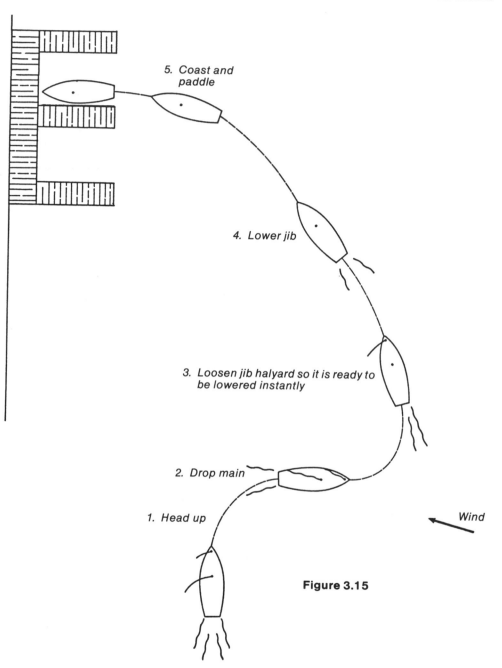

5. Coast and paddle

4. Lower jib

3. Loosen jib halyard so it is ready to be lowered instantly

2. Drop main

1. Head up

Wind

Figure 3.15

An alternative and somewhat trickier solution would be to head up and drop your main a good distance from the docks and come in on the jib alone (Figure 3.15). The jib halyard should be loosened so that it may be dropped instantly, and you should plan to drop it early enough so that you need only a few paddle strokes to make it into the slip.

If your boat has an engine, start the engine well away from the docks, head up into the wind, drop both sails, and motor in. Never attempt to make a downwind landing with the sails up (Figure 3.16)!

Figure 3.16 *Never attempt a downwind landing with the sails up!*

Once you get your boat into the dock, the best way to secure it is to use a bow line and a stern line to hold the boat close to the dock and *springlines* fore and aft to keep the boat from moving forward or backward (Figure 3.17). Notice how the after springline prevents the boat from surging forward into the dock.

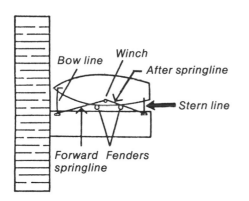

Figure 3.17 *Notice how the after springline prevents the boat from surging forward into the dock.*

DON'T LOSE THE BOAT: ESSENTIAL KNOTS

It is quite embarrassing, not to mention alarming, to return to your moored boat after an absence to find that your knots have come undone. It's almost as embarrassing to invite guests down for a sail and then have to spend an hour trying to untie an overly thorough knot.

There are a few important knots that you should know, each of which has a particular application. These knots have evolved over the years to be quickly tied, absolutely reliable, easy to untie, and easily recognized by other sailors.

Belaying a Line to a Cleat

Cleats have been used for centuries by seamen to secure boats to a dock, as well as securing halyards and other running rigging on the boat. It is a good idea to know the correct way for belaying a line to a cleat. (See Figure 3.18.)

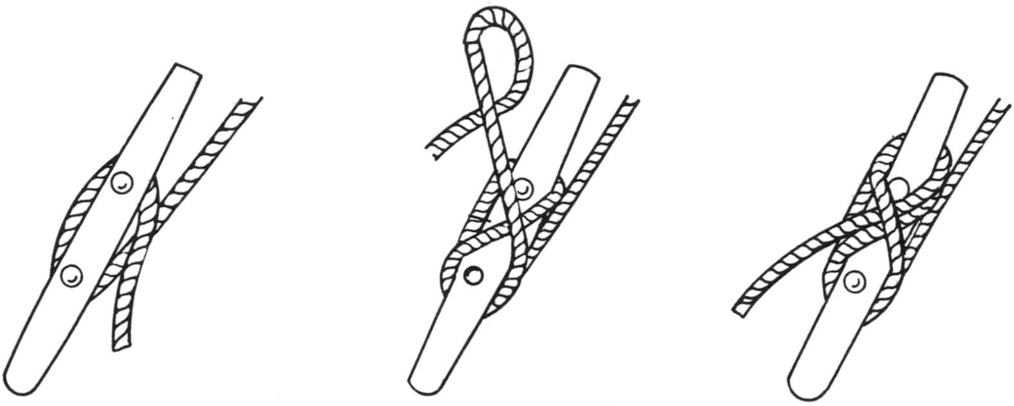

Figure 3.18   Belaying a line

Clove Hitch

A *clove hitch* is the quickest way to secure a line to a piling. If you are very fond of your boat, then after tying the clove hitch, you will take the free end and tie a half hitch (simple overhand knot) back on the line (Figure 3.19). The reason for this is that a clove hitch may, in time, unwind if equal or almost equal loads are not maintained on both ends of the line. By tying a hitch back onto the standing part of the line, this problem is avoided.

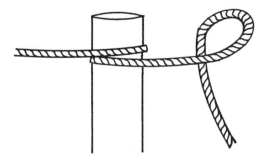

Figure 3.19   Clove hitch

Two Half Hitches

Two half hitches is one of the simplest and most effective knots you can tie. You tie one half hitch, then tie another half hitch in the same direction. When you do this correctly, you have tied a clove hitch back on the line. Two half hitches can be tied and untied with tension on the line (see Figure 3.20).

Figure 3.20   Two half hitches

Bowline

The bowline is a knot all sailors should know (see Figure 3.21). It is the best knot for making a loop that will not slip but can easily be untied once tension is off the line.

These are the most important knots, and there will be times when you need to tie them quickly and correctly—sometimes in the dark. So it is a good idea to learn them well. Try tying them with your eyes shut. Practicing tying knots is often more fun than watching TV and invariably more satisfying.

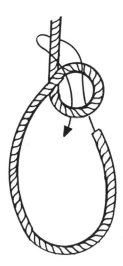

Figure 3.21   Bowline

4

SAIL TRIM AND BALANCE

ow that you have gotten safely out of the mooring area and know about the points of sail, how to tack, and how to jibe, we should talk a bit about balance.

BALANCE

If you have done any sailing before, you have probably experienced, especially on windy days, the following:

There you are sailing close-hauled, heeling over, and in order to make the boat sail straight, you have to hold the tiller substantially to windward. You feel an uncomfortable pressure on the tiller and the boat is going slower than it should, but you're used to it. If you were to let go of the tiller, the boat would head up to weather (windward). This tendency to head up to windward is known as *weather helm* (Figure 4.1).

Weather helm is a drag. It is a drag because, in order to make the boat sail straight (which you must do if you want to get anywhere), you have to compensate by holding the tiller to windward. If you are holding the tiller to windward, then the rudder no longer slices through the water but is at an angle to your course and so acts like a brake or a drag. So, quite literally, weather helm is a drag.

It's better to balance your boat so that it tends to go straight all the time. Here are a few concepts to help you understand how to do this.

First, it turns out that the more you heel, the more weather helm you get (the more the boat tries to head up). To see why, consider only the component of force that pushes forward (the driving force). Think of it as the hand of the wind god pushing forward at a point halfway up the mast (Figures 4.2a and 4.2b). So clearly, one way to reduce weather helm is to do your best to minimize heeling. Get as much body weight to windward as you can, for instance.

We will now look into how to keep your boat balanced at all times. There are three

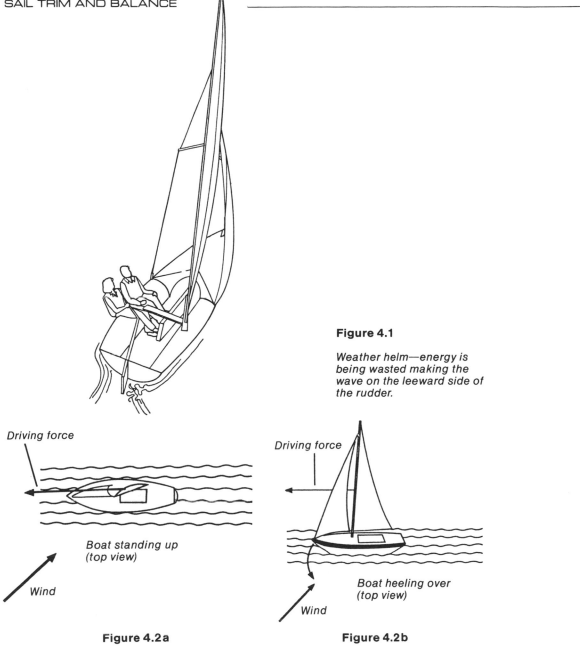

Figure 4.1

Weather helm—energy is being wasted making the wave on the leeward side of the rudder.

Driving force

Boat standing up (top view)

Wind

Figure 4.2a

Driving force

Boat heeling over (top view)

Wind

Figure 4.2b

distinct cases to deal with. First, you would like to have your boat naturally balanced under average conditions, say 6 to 12 knots of wind. Second, when it is windier you are likely to heel more and need to eliminate the weather helm that this would create. And third, you may be perfectly balanced for whatever conditions you happen to be sailing in when a gust of wind comes along and suddenly heels you over, increasing your weather helm. You want to be able to deal with that, too.

The principle by which you control the balance of your helm is the same in each of these cases. A couple of useful concepts will lead us to this principle.

One such concept is that we can consider the force of the wind acting on a sail to be equivalent to the force of the wind acting at one particular point. This unique point is called the *center of effort*. The mainsail has a center of effort, the jib has a center of effort, and the entire sailplan has a center of effort. For the purpose of talking about balance, we can pretend that the wind acting on the sails acts at the center of effort.

The second useful concept is the idea of the *pivot point*, about which the boat turns. The location of this pivot point is determined by the design of the hull and the keel and is given careful consideration by most sailboat designers. The pivot point is also called the *center of lateral resistance* (Figure 4.3).

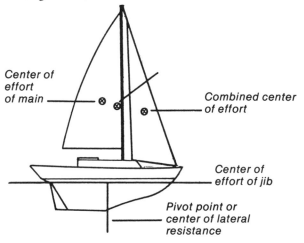

Center of
effort
of main

Combined center
of effort

Center of
effort of jib

Pivot point or
center of lateral
resistance

Figure 4.3 *Remember that the force of the wind acting on the sails has a forward component and a lateral component. Now consider only the lateral component. Imagine the finger of the wind god pushing at the center of effort.*

Remember that the force of the wind acting on the sails has a forward component and a lateral component. For now consider only the lateral component. Imagine the finger of the wind god pushing at the center of effort.

If you were to sail with just the main, then the main's center of effort would be the only center of effort. Since this center of effort would lie behind the pivot point, it would push the stern downwind and pivot the boat up into the wind, thereby creating weather helm.

If, on the other hand, you sail with just the jib, the bow will tend to get blown downwind. When a boat tends to turn downwind of its own accord, it is said to have *lee helm*.

Lee helm is the opposite of weather helm. Doing something to increase lee helm will decrease weather helm and conversely. From this it follows that if you do something to move the center of effort forward, you will decrease weather helm.

Now to the application of the principle. Suppose that after reading this book you go out and buy a $50,000 sloop. You take it out and find that when sailing close-hauled or on a close reach, even when the wind is blowing only 12 knots or so and you are not heeling much, you have uncomfortable weather helm (as might often be the case).

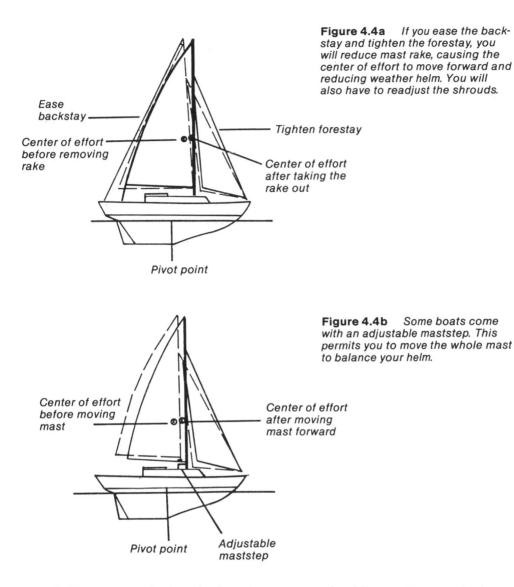

Figure 4.4a *If you ease the backstay and tighten the forestay, you will reduce mast rake, causing the center of effort to move forward and reducing weather helm. You will also have to readjust the shrouds.*

Ease backstay

Tighten forestay

Center of effort before removing rake

Center of effort after taking the rake out

Pivot point

Figure 4.4b *Some boats come with an adjustable maststep. This permits you to move the whole mast to balance your helm.*

Center of effort before moving mast

Center of effort after moving mast forward

Pivot point

Adjustable maststep

Before you take the boat back to the store, you should try tuning your rigging to eliminate the weather helm. To eliminate weather helm, you want to move the center of effort forward permanently. One way to do this is to tilt the mast forward or remove the *rake* (rake is tilt aft) (Figures 4.4a and 4.4b).

If you ease the backstay and tighten the forestay, you will reduce mast rake, causing the center of effort to move forward and reducing weather helm. You may also have to readjust the shrouds. Some boats come with an adjustable mast step. This permits you to move the whole mast to adjust the balance of your helm.

A matter of only a few inches in either the mast rake or in the position of the mast step can make a significant difference in the balance of the boat. By using these two techniques, you should be able to get your boat properly balanced for average conditions. Please note, however, that this discussion assumes your sails are perfectly trimmed. If, for example, you were sailing with your mainsail overtrimmed and your jib out too far, your center of effort would be farther aft than it should be, and you would have weather helm even if your rig were perfectly tuned.

REEFING

Suppose now that you have your boat well balanced. You're out sailing and it's a beautiful day, but gradually, the wind is building. As it builds, you find you heel more and, as a result, your weather helm increases to the point of discomfort. You take down your *genoa* (large jib) and put up your *working jib* (small jib) so you don't heel so much. That helps, but as the wind keeps building you heel more, and soon you have too much weather helm again. The problem is you've got too much sail up for the conditions, and it's time to *reef*. Reefing means shortening or reducing the area of sail you're carrying. Invariably, you reef the main.

There are two principal methods in use these days for reefing a marconi main.

With *roller reefing*, you ease the main halyard as you rotate the boom, which effectively rolls the sail up on the boom. When you think you have rolled enough sail around the boom, tighten the halyard again and sheet in.

Slab reefing is a fairly recent improvement on a much older system (Figures 4.5a and 4.5b). It is better than roller reefing in that it is not only faster and easier, but when you are finished reefing, your sail has a perfect shape, which it does not have in the case of roller reefing.

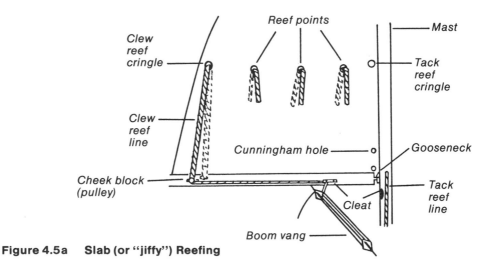

Figure 4.5a   Slab (or "jiffy") Reefing

The clew reef line is secured to the boom opposite the cheek block. The tack reef line may be a specific line for that purpose, or it may be the same tackle used for the cunningham, or it may be a "horn" fitting, which can securely hold the tack reef cringle. Reef points are simply three-foot lengths of line passed through cringles (holes) in the sail and knotted so they stay there.

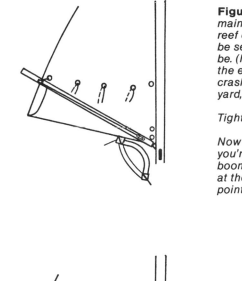

Figure 4.5b *To reef, ease the boom vang and mainsheet and lower the halyard until the tack reef cringle can be easily slid over the horn or be secured by the tack reef line as the case may be. (Note: If you have a topping lift attached to the end of the boom to keep the boom from crashing onto the deck when you lower the halyard, make sure it's on and secured, etc., first.)*

Tighten the clew reef line hard and cleat it.

Now retension the halyard and sheet in—you're reefed. At your leisure, retighten the boom vang and then furl the excess material at the foot of the sail and tie it with the reef points.

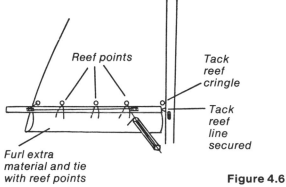

Reef points

Tack reef cringle

Tack reef line secured

Furl extra material and tie with reef points

Figure 4.6

Whichever reefing technique you use, a boat with a reefed main looks like the boat shown in Figure 4.6.

Reefing not only reduces heeling, which cuts down on weather helm, but also takes sail off the "back" of the main. This causes the center of effort to move forward, further reducing weather helm. And sailing upwind on a windy day, a reefed boat will sail more upright, more comfortably, faster, and more enjoyably than would a similar boat without a reef.

Here is a good technique for determining when it is time to reef: If you find yourself wondering whether or not you should reef, it's time to reef.

A fishermen's reef—as opposed to a sailor's reef—is the technique of luffing your main when it's windy to reduce heeling and get the center of effort forward. This type of reef is very hard on the sail; I don't recommend it unless you get four months off per year and like to spend the time mending nets and sewing sails.

So far, we have discussed techniques for reducing weather helm by moving the center of effort forward. Moving the pivot point aft would have the same effect in terms of reducing weather helm, and while one cannot easily do this on a keelboat, one can on a small centerboard (Figure 4.7).

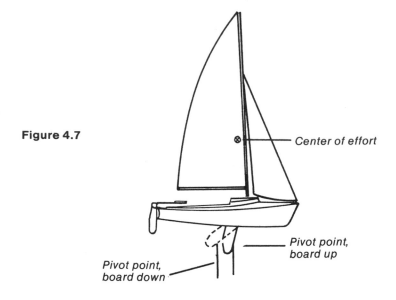

Figure 4.7

Center of effort

Pivot point,
board up

Pivot point,
board down

Notice how raising the centerboard slightly moves the pivot point aft. This effectively puts more sail forward of the pivot, which holds the bow downwind.

Beating in strong wind, a boat with its centerboard slightly raised is phenomenally faster and easier to sail than one with its board all the way down.

Sitting farther aft in the boat would also move the pivot aft by getting the stern farther down in the water.

We have discussed how to balance your boat for average conditions and some techniques for maintaining that balance when it blows. We should now talk about how to deal with gusts of wind that tend to heel you over suddenly and how to avoid weather helm and the associated chaos that can result.

Reaching (close-, beam-, or broad-reaching), you're usually on the course you want to be on, heading for some destination, and you don't want the weather helm from a surprise gust heading you up and getting you off course. With experience, you will be able to see these gusts coming and react instantly. In any case, as quickly as you can, you should ease out your main. Easing your main in a gust will minimize heeling and let the jib draw harder than the main, thus minimizing weather helm. When the gust has passed, sheet your main back in. With a little practice, you can use your main as a shock absorber and maintain perfect balance at all times.

When you're beating, a gust can also heel you over and head you up, but the fact is that in a gust you *can* sail higher. Since higher is the way you want to go when beating, you should take advantage of the gust and let the boat "feather" up. Be careful not to head up so high that you luff and lose speed. If it's a very strong gust, you can ease your main as a shock absorber as you feather up. Then trim it back in.

How is it that a gust enables you to point higher? Consider that you sail on the apparent wind, which is the true wind shifted forward by the headwind created by your boat speed. The true wind is therefore always aft of the apparent wind. A gust means more true wind so the true wind is then a greater contribution to the apparent wind than it was before. So in a gust, the apparent wind shifts closer to the true wind,

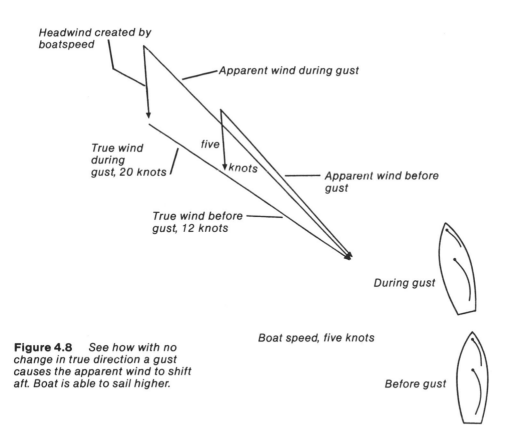

Headwind created by boatspeed

Apparent wind during gust

True wind during gust, 20 knots

five knots

Apparent wind before gust

True wind before gust, 12 knots

During gust

Boat speed, five knots

Before gust

Figure 4.8 *See how with no change in true direction a gust causes the apparent wind to shift aft. Boat is able to sail higher.*

or aft. When the wind shifts aft, you can head up (Figure 4.8). See how, with no change in true wind direction, a gust causes the apparent wind to shift aft. The boat is able to sail higher.

Beating in gusty air is one of the more difficult skills to master—particularly the proper easing and trimming of the main to maintain balance through gusts and lulls. An exercise that may help you master this skill is sailing without the rudder. Try it at first in a gentle wind. Don't try it in traffic. If you lash or hold your tiller centered, you find that when you trim in the main, the center of effort moves aft, you heel some, and the boat heads up. If you ease the main, the center of effort moves forward, you heel less, and the boat falls off.

Indeed, when it's windy, the boat will not fall off unless you ease the main. Probably the most common cause of port-starboard collisions (the worst kind) among beginning racers is trying to fall off behind the other boat to avoid collision and forgetting to ease the main. The boat heels more, develops more weather helm, and will not fall off regardless of what you do with the rudder—embarrassing and expensive.

Sailboats often heel to leeward, and as we discussed near the beginning of this section, heeling creates weather helm. Sailboat designers know this, and to

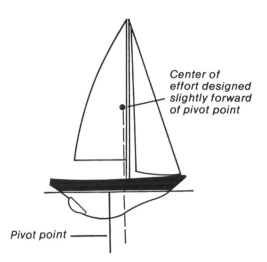

Figure 4.9

Center of effort designed slightly forward of pivot point

Pivot point

compensate for what would otherwise be weather helm they design the center of effort to be slightly forward of the pivot point (Figure 4.9).

This means that if you do not heel, as in very light wind, you will have lee helm. Like weather helm, lee helm is a drag. Therefore, in light wind you should sit to leeward to make the boat heel and keep it balanced.

When you make the boat heel in this fashion, the force of gravity causes the sails to fall into approximately the correct shape for the occasional wind molecule that crashes into them. This is effective when there is otherwise not enough wind to give shape to the sails.

SAIL-SHAPE CONTROL

By now, you have probably observed that most of the problems associated with excessive heeling when sailing upwind result from the wind imparting too much power to the sails. In the previous section, we discussed reefing as one method of reducing power in order to control heeling and balance. We will now discuss techniques for altering your sail shape in order to control more accurately the amount of power the wind delivers to your sails regardless of wind strength. Let's look again at how power is generated when sailing upwind (Figure 4.10).

Wind

Figure 4.10 *Bernoulli's principle acting on the wing-shaped sails creates drive when sailing upwind. It should come as no surprise that sails with more curve, or draft, generate greater power, and sails with less draft generate less power.*

It is the curved shape of the sail that creates drive when sailing upwind. It should come as no surprise, then, that sails with more curve, or *draft*, generate greater power and sails with less draft generate less power.

To the extent that we can control the draft of the sails, we can control the power the wind delivers to them. In strong wind, we can minimize what would otherwise be too much power by flattening the sails. In light air, we need the maximum power the sails can generate, so we want full, round sails.

There are a few specific methods for controlling the shape of your sails, but first let's look at two ways the sailmaker builds curve into sails (see Figures 4.11a and 4.11b).

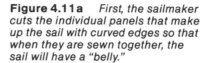

Figure 4.11a *First, the sailmaker cuts the individual panels that make up the sail with curved edges so that when they are sewn together, the sail will have a "belly."*

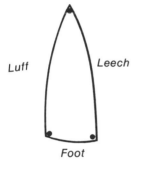

Luff

Leech

Foot

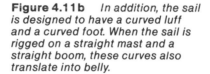

Figure 4.11b *In addition, the sail is designed to have a curved luff and a curved foot. When the sail is rigged on a straight mast and a straight boom, these curves also translate into belly.*

There is one additional aspect of sail construction that helps us understand how to control sail shape while underway. The sailmaker always arranges the cloth so that when the sail is finished, the fibers that make up the cloth run parallel and perpendicular to the leech. Since the fibers run along the leech, the leech can't stretch.

Observe, however, what happens when you put more tension on the luff by tightening either the halyard or the downhaul or cunningham (Figure 4.12a) or when you put more tension on the foot by tightening the outhaul (Figure 4.12b).

Tightening the luff by any of the above methods stretches it and in so doing draws the cloth forward, reducing draft in the sail. Any sail can be flattened by tightening its

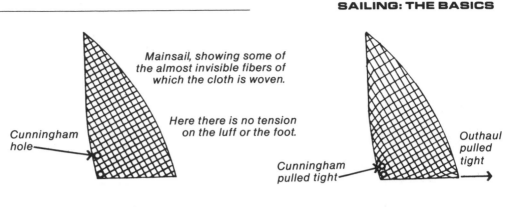

Figure 4.12a

Mainsail, showing some of
the almost invisible fibers of
which the cloth is woven.

Here there is no tension
on the luff or the foot.

Cunningham
hole

Figure 4.12b

Cunningham
pulled tight

Outhaul
pulled
tight

luff. Stretching the foot by tightening the outhaul also takes some draft out of the sail.

If you are not yet convinced, try this experiment with a handkerchief: Pull along one edge, and you will observe that it stretches very little since the fibers run parallel to the edge as they do in the leech of a sail. Now pull on diagonally opposite corners while someone holds one of the other corners. As the cloth stretches (corresponding to tightening the luff or the foot), observe what happens to the rest of the handkerchief.

A main, flattened by tightening the cunningham and outhaul, gives less heeling and more comfort in strong wind (see Figure 4.13).

Figure 4.13

This full main will provide
the greatest drive in light
air.

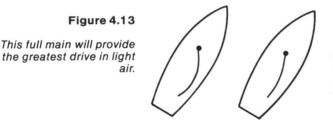

This main, flattened by tightening the cunningham and
outhaul, would result in less
heeling and more comfort in
strong wind.

Some boats (Solings and Sonars, for example) have an adjustable backstay or some other means of bending the mast while underway. A bent mast matches the curve that the sailmaker builds into the luff of a mainsail and so reduces the draft (Figure 4.14). At the same time, bending brings the top of the mast closer to the end of the boom, thereby easing some of the tension on the leech and reducing the amount by which the leech hooks to windward (Figures 4.15a and 4.15b). Notice that you can only bend a mast by tightening the backstay on a boat with a *fractional rig*, a rig where the forestay does not go all the way to the *masthead*, or top of the mast.

It is as important to flatten the jib when beating in strong wind as it is to flatten the main. One of the things you do to the jib when it's windy is to tighten its luff. You do this by pulling the halyard tighter or by tightening the jib downhaul if your boat has one.

You can also control the amount of draft in the jib by adjusting the jib fairleads.

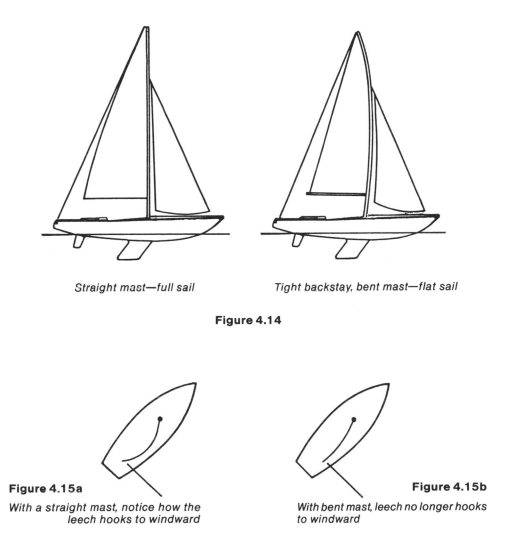

Straight mast—full sail

Tight backstay, bent mast—flat sail

Figure 4.14

Figure 4.15a

With a straight mast, notice how the
leech hooks to windward

Figure 4.15b

With bent mast, leech no longer hooks
to windward

With the fairlead forward, pulling in the sheet pulls more down on the leech, less back on the foot. So the sail has a big, full curve in it. This gives maximum power for light-wind sailing (Figures 4.16a and 4.16b). With the fairlead aft, the sheet pulls more back on the foot, less down on the leech. So the foot is flat, and since the leech has less tension, it will twist off to leeward near the head. Therefore, the bottom of the sail will draw more strongly than the top, so the force is lower and you heel less, all of which is helpful in strong wind (Figure 4.16c).

The third adjustment you make to control the shape of the jib while beating concerns how tight you pull in your sheet. In light air, you need a full sail for drive so you cannot afford to trim it in too tight. When it is windy, though, crank the jib in tight. This not only flattens the sail more, but in so doing enables you to point higher and heel less. Also, tightening the jib moves the center of effort forward, which in strong wind reduces weather helm (Figure 4.17).

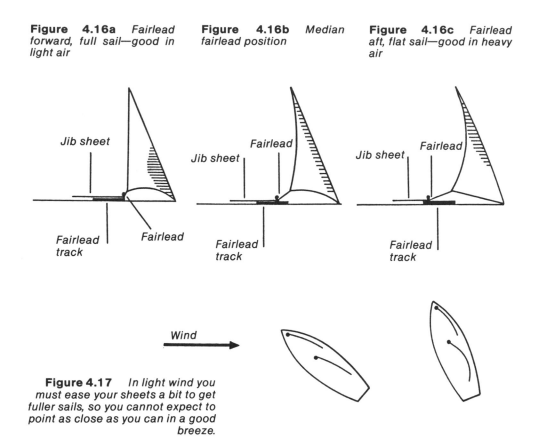

Figure 4.16a *Fairlead forward, full sail—good in light air*

Figure 4.16b *Median fairlead position*

Figure 4.16c *Fairlead aft, flat sail—good in heavy air*

Figure 4.17 *In light wind you must ease your sheets a bit to get fuller sails, so you cannot expect to point as close as you can in a good breeze.*

SAIL TRIM WHEN RUNNING AND REACHING

Now that we have discussed various methods of tuning your sails to match the wind strength when beating, let's talk about tuning your sails when reaching and running.

When sailing on a reach or a run, you can handle more wind, even when it is quite windy, so it is no longer necessary to have sails as flat as when beating. Also, when you're off the wind, bending your mast does nothing but reduce your effective sail area, so your mast should be straight.

As you fall off to a reach and ease the sails, the mainsheet no longer pulls almost directly down on the boom as it does when beating, so the tendency is for the boom to lift and the sail to *twist*. Twist means that the bottom part of the sail is closer to the centerline of the boat than the top part of the sail. This means that either the foot area is in too tight or the head area is out too far; but obviously, the whole sail can never be set at the perfect angle to the wind when this is the case. The jib also tends to twist when on a reach, and this reduces its effectiveness, too.

There are two adjustments you can make to reduce twist in the main when reaching and one adjustment that will do the same for the jib.

The main cannot twist if the boom does not lift. To hold the boom down when off the wind, make sure the boom vang is tight and ease the traveler to leeward. Easing the traveler to leeward causes the mainsheet to pull somewhat more down on the end of the boom than it would if the traveler were centered (Figures 4.18a and 4.18b).

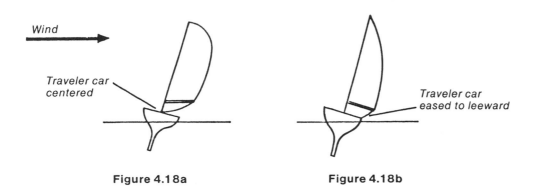

Figure 4.18a   **Figure 4.18b**

See how much more effectively the mainsheet holds down the end of the boom with the traveler car out to leeward.

To take the twist out of the jib when reaching, some boats have an esoteric piece of equipment called a *barber-hauler*. (Solings and a few other high-performance boats have them.) The jib sheets reeve first through the barber-haulers, then through the fairleads. When beating, the barber-haulers are slack. They ride on the jib sheets and have no effect. When reaching, however, you can draw the barber-haulers out to the rail. This then becomes the new sheeting position for the jib, and the result is a better airfoil when reaching (Figure 4.19).

Figure 4.19

SUMMARY OF BALANCE AND SAIL-SHAPE CONTROL

These sections on balance, reefing, and sail-shape control are designed to refine your understanding of the intricate relationships between wind, sails, boat, and water. Understanding the information in these sections is important to becoming an excellent sailor regardless of whether your interests tend toward racing, cruising, or daysailing. On the other hand, there is a great deal of new information here, which is nearly impossible for a newcomer to memorize all at once, so a summary is in order.

Most of the issues dealt with in these sections have to do with maintaining control of the boat regardless of wind strength and other conditions. A boat with excessive weather helm is not in complete control because it will not readily bear off when you need it to. Excessive heeling also makes it more difficult for skipper and crew to keep their balance on the boat and more difficult to see to leeward under the sails. A boat that continually gets knocked over in gusts, rounds up, slows down, etc., is also out of control by any reasonable definition.

Most of these problems occur while sailing upwind, as this is when lateral (heeling) force is the greatest. Sailing upwind (beating or close-reaching), the key to maintaining control is balance (i.e., either neutral helm so that the boat would continue straight if you let go of the tiller, or a slight amount of weather helm so the boat would head up slowly if you let go of the tiller) at all times.

Let's go through the steps you would take to maintain balance as wind steadily increases: In light air, use crew weight to heel the boat and set your sails to be full and powerful. As the wind builds, move crew weight to windward and begin to flatten your sails to depower them and maintain balance. As the wind builds further, drop genoa and put up jib (if appropriate) and/or flatten sails as much as necessary to maintain neutral or slight weather helm. As the wind builds to the point where it is difficult to maintain a balanced helm by flattening sails, reef the main. If the wind builds beyond that point, you probably should not be out there (see Chapter 10, "Heavy Weather Sailing").

In gusty conditions, you must keep your hand on the mainsheet or main traveler so you can immediately ease the main in a gust to keep the boat balanced and under control and bring the sail back in when the gust has passed. In addition, when beating, you can almost always feather up (point higher) during a gust.

Here is a summary of the adjustments you might make to control your sail shape under varying conditions. The list does not tell you exactly how much to loosen or tighten each line for each set of conditions—a thing better learned while sailing than while reading. To the extent that you make these adjustments, however, you will find that you sail not only faster, but more enjoyably and safely as well.

Beating—Strong Wind

Tighten cunningham and outhaul; tighten jib downhaul and/or jib halyard; move jib fairlead aft and sheet jib in tight; tighten backstay; ease the main traveller; get as much crew weight to windward as possible. Note: In waves, you cannot point quite as high. Ease your sheets a crack and sail with both leeches twisted open a bit more.

Beating—Light Wind

Ease cunningham and outhaul; ease tension on jib luff; move jib fairlead forward and don't sheet it in too tight; ease backstay to straighten mast; use your weight to make the boat heel to leeward.

Reaching or Running—Any Wind

Ease cunningham and outhaul; ease jib downhaul; ease backstay; ease main traveler to leeward and tighten barber-haulers if you use them. Keep the boat level.

HULL SPEED

A keel boat is often referred to as a *displacement* boat because it usually behaves like one; that is, it plows through the water as in Figure 4.20, instead of *surfing* (riding the waves like a surfboard), or *planing* (skimming across the surface like a speedboat).

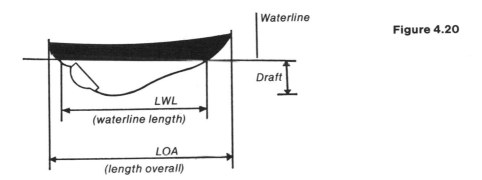

Figure 4.20

Any boat that behaves like a displacement boat (neither surfing nor planing) has a maximum speed it cannot exceed regardless of how much wind or engine power is applied. This maximum potential speed is known as *hull speed*.

Hull speed says nothing about how fast a boat will go in less than maximum speed conditions. Under lesser conditions, speed is determined mainly by sail area (which increases it), and by the "wetted surface" (Figure 4.21) of the hull (which decreases it).

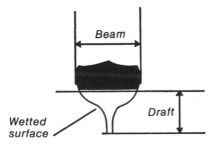

Figure 4.21

Hull speed, though, is the *maximum* speed a displacement boat can attain and is determined only by the "LWL" ("load waterline" or waterline length). Here's why:

As a boat moves through the water it makes waves. The faster it travels, the longer the waves become (Figure 4.22). Well, there is a rule about waves, and that is that the speed of a wave is determined exactly by its length. As a wave's length increases, its speed increases. In fact, the speed of a water wave (in knots) can be found by multiplying the square root of its length (in feet) by 1.4.

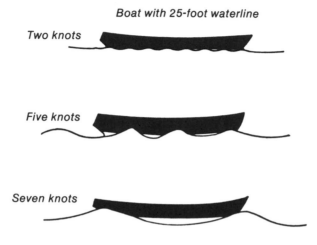

Figure 4.22 *At hull speed a boat drops into the trough of its wave and can go no faster than that wave.*

So as a boat moving through the water gains speed, the waves it creates increase in length until the boat is making a wave as long as its LWL. At this speed, the boat is trapped in its wave and can go no faster than that wave. This is the maximum speed the boat can attain, its hull speed, and it can be approximated by the following formula.

$$\text{hull speed (in knots)} = 1.4 \times \sqrt{\text{LWL (in feet)}}$$

In the fairly typical example above, a keelboat with a 25-foot LWL should have a maximum attainable speed of

$$1.4 \times \sqrt{25} = 1.4 \times 5 = 7 \text{ knots.}$$

Some boats are light displacement and have a flat bottom aft so that when there is enough wind they can lift out of the water and plane, like a hydroplane. When a boat begins planing, it is no longer displacing water and no longer making waves. When a boat stops making waves, its speed is technically unlimited.

Cruising keelboats virtually never plane, but when a sea is running and you're sailing on a broad reach with plenty of wind, even a 30-foot cruising boat may surf at speeds as high as 12 knots for short periods.

Upwind, however, boats will neither plane nor surf but will be limited by their hull speed. So when the wind builds and it's getting near time to reef, you should reef because you're probably going hull speed anyway and you gain nothing by not reefing.

USING WIND SHIFTS

Up to now, we have been talking about the wind as if it were steady, but the fact is that it is often shifty. When the wind does shift, however, it usually shifts within reliable limits. From the average direction the wind will *veer* (shift clockwise) and *back* (shift counterclockwise) a maximum of maybe 30 degrees each on even the shiftiest of days (Figure 4.23).

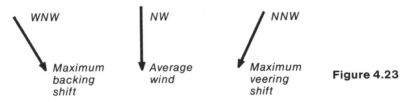

WNW — Maximum backing shift

NW — Average wind

NNW — Maximum veering shift

Figure 4.23

A northwest wind may cycle slowly back and forth between north northwest and west northwest, taking maybe 10 or 15 minutes to complete each cycle.

Note: A northwest wind blows *from* the northwest.

Now let's look at what happens when a boat beating to an upwind destination gets a veering (clockwise) shift (Figure 4.24). To a boat on starboard tack, a veering

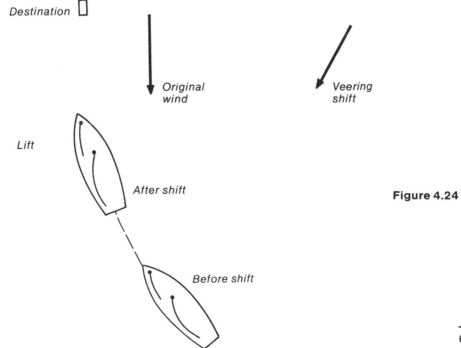

Destination

Original wind

Veering shift

Lift

After shift

Before shift

Figure 4.24

shift is a shift aft, and the skipper is able to head up and point closer to his destination. He is still beating at the same angle to the wind as before, but the wind has shifted aft, enabling him to head up. Such a shift is called *lift*, because when you get it, you can sail closer to where you want to go.

To a boat on port tack, however, a veering shift is a shift forward (a *header*), and the skipper must fall off and point even farther from his destination to keep his sails full (Figure 4.25).

Figure 4.25

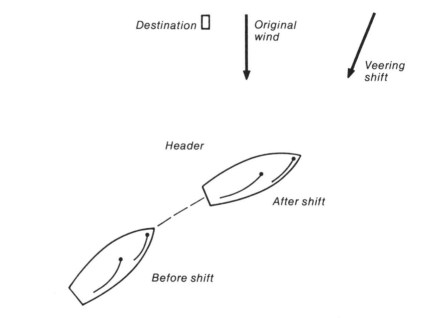

So a veering shift is a header for port tack and a lift for starboard tack. Similarly, a backing shift would be a header for starboard tack and a lift for port tack. In other words, a shift that is a header for one tack is a lift for the other tack. Therefore, when you get a header, you should tack.

Imagine that you're sailing close-hauled on starboard tack, beating to your upwind destination, and you sight a tree dead ahead.

A bit later, still sailing the best close-hauled course you can, you notice that you can no longer point high enough to head for the tree. You have gotten a header.

The best thing to do at this point is to tack and be lifted closer to your destination on the other tack (Figure 4.26).

In general, when beating upwind, you should try to tack on the headers. If you do this, you can get upwind faster than if you tack arbitrarily, and in fact, you get upwind faster than you would if the wind were perfectly steady.

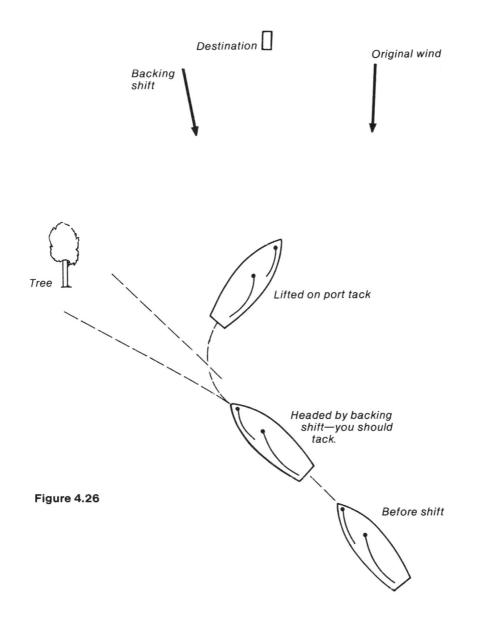

Destination

Original wind

Backing
shift

Tree

Lifted on port tack

Headed by backing
shift—you should
tack.

Figure 4.26

Before shift

5

RULES OF THE ROAD

essels of any description operating in inland waters, or at sea, are bound by a set of laws, the Rules of the Road, designed to prevent collisions at sea. In any potential collision situation they tell you which boats are *privileged* and which are *burdened*.

A *burdened* vessel is required to alter course, slow, or stop in order to avoid collision. Also, the skipper of a burdened boat should take evasive action early enough so that the skipper of the privileged vessel understands his intentions and is not confused by them.

A *privileged* vessel is required to maintain course and speed and remain alert to the possibility that the burdened vessel's skipper might not know what he is doing. (In fact, one of the rules, called the "General Prudential Rule," states: "Notwithstanding any of the other rules, avoid collison." It is small satisfaction to have been the privileged vessel in a collision and have the money sent to your next of kin.)

With this in mind, let's look at the rules governing meetings between two sailboats, as shown in Figures 5.1 to 5.3.

Figure 5.1   Sailboats meeting sailboats—overtaking situation

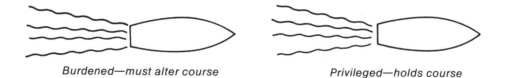

Burdened—must alter course   *Privileged—holds course*

If one boat is overtaking the other, the boat being overtaken is privileged and the overtaking boat is burdened. (You're not supposed to crash into anybody from behind.)

Figure 5.2   Sailboats meeting sailboats—opposite tacks

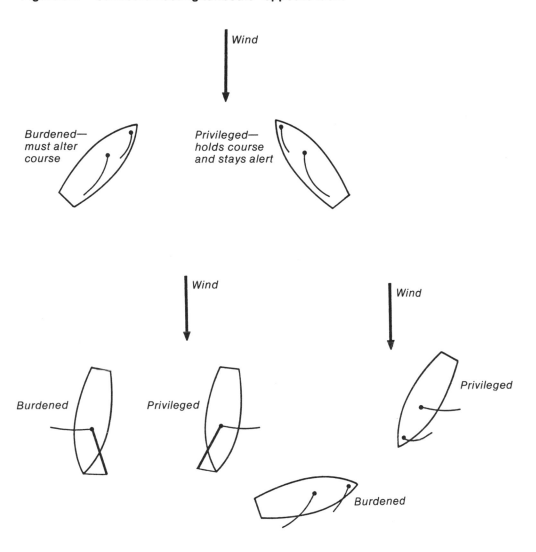

If two boats are on opposite tacks, the one on starboard tack is privileged; the one on port tack is burdened.

There are three rules formulated to work in order. In any potential collision situation, check first to see if it is an overtaking situation. If it is, Rule #1 resolves it. If it is not an overtaking situation, check to see if the two boats are on opposite tacks. If they are, Rule #2 resolves the situation. If they are not on opposite tacks, then they must be on the same tack; use Rule #3.

Figure 5.3   Sailboats meeting sailboats—same tack

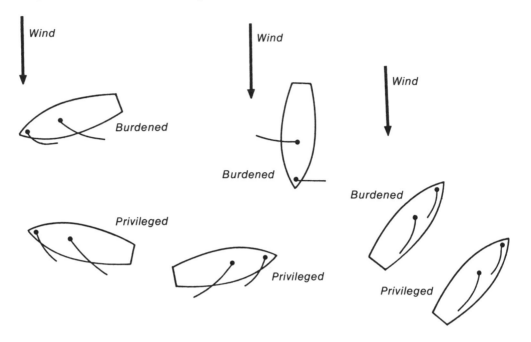

If two boats are on the same tack, the one to leeward (on the same side as the other one's mainsail) is privileged. The boat to windward is burdened.

If your boat is running under auxiliary motor, then, for the purposes of the Rules of the Road, you are considered a motorboat, even if your sails are up. So you should know the two rules for motorboats meeting other motorboats (Figure 5.4).

Figure 5.4   Motorboats meeting motorboats

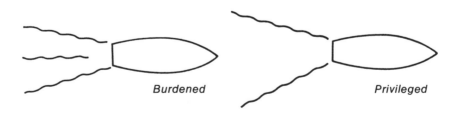

If one boat is overtaking the other, the boat being overtaken is privileged, and the overtaking boat is burdened. In all other meetings between two motorboats, there is a "danger zone," an arc extending from dead ahead to "two points abaft the starboard beam."

Before the circle was divided into 360 degrees, mariners divided it into 32 *points*, each point being 11¼ degrees. Bearings were then described in terms of how many points forward or *abaft* (behind) the beam and how many points off dead ahead or dead astern an object was (Figure 5.5). Now if you're in a motorboat and another motorboat is approaching on a potential collision course in your "danger zone," watch out: He is privileged and you are burdened. You must take evasive action. It

Figure 5.5

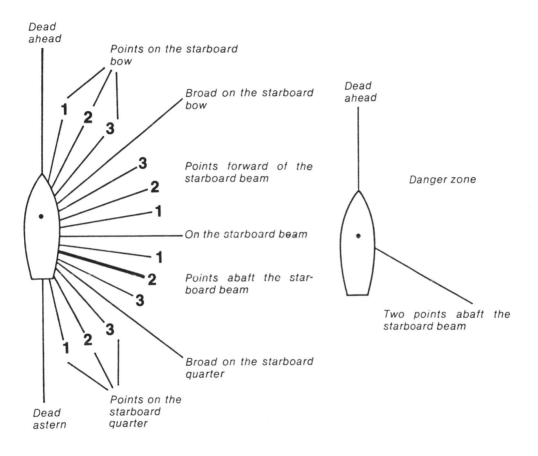

boils down to the motorboat on the *right* having the *right* of way (is privileged) (Figure 5.6).

Note: A vessel approaching from more than two points abaft the beam on starboard is considered overtaking and must keep clear.

Figure 5.6 Motorboats meeting motorboats

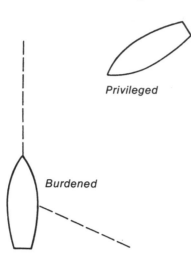

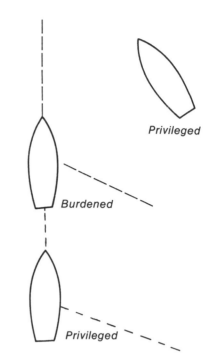

SAILBOATS MEETING MOTORBOATS

When a sailboat and a motorboat are on a potential collision course, the sailboat is privileged and the motorboat is burdened *except in the following cases*:

1. If the sailboat is overtaking the motorboat, then the motorboat is privileged and the sailboat is burdened.
2. If the motorboat is anchored, aground, or capsized, it is privileged over other vessels.
3. If you're sailing any vessel and a large commercial tanker is coming up the harbor, stay clear! The official rule is that a vessel that cannot safely navigate outside the deep water channel is privileged over any vessel that can (Figure 5.7). Moreover, whether or not you are in a deep water channel, a large tanker needs more than a mile to stop. It cannot easily turn, and often the captain

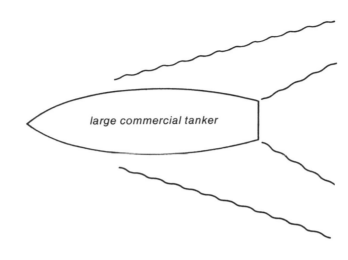

Sailboat

Figure 5.7

can't even see a small boat under his bow. Also, tankers are always moving faster than you think they are, so take evasive action *early* when you see one heading your way.

SAILING AT NIGHT

Vessels operating at night are obligated under both *International* and *Inland Rules of the Road* to show *running lights*, which, unlike car lights, are designed only to be seen and do nothing at all to help you see.

The basic running light configuration consists of a 10-point (112.5°) red port light, a 10-point (112.5°) green starboard light, and a 12-point (135°) white stern light. Any sailboat operating at night must show this basic configuration of running lights. A boat under seven meters in length meets legal requirements by carrying a flashlight to indicate its approach to another vessel (Figure 5.8).

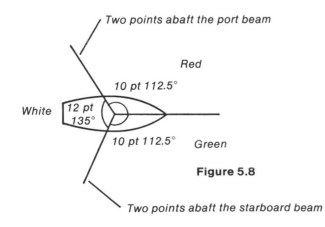

Two points abaft the port beam

Red

10 pt 112.5°

White   12 pt 135°

10 pt 112.5°   Green

Figure 5.8

Two points abaft the starboard beam

The port and starboard side lights may be combined into a 20-point combination bow light, and a boat under 12 meters in length may combine all three required lights into a combination masthead light. The advantage to such combinations is that reducing the number of lightbulbs reduces the power drain on your batteries, which, on a small sailboat, is an important consideration.

The idea behind running lights is that when you see another boat at night you can tell by the color of the light which sector of the other boat you are looking at, and from that determine whether or not you are in a crossing situation and what, if anything, you should do about it.

For example, sailing at night, if you see a green light off your port bow, you are looking at the starboard bow of a sailboat (assuming that it is properly lit) and you and it are likely to be in a crossing situation. Since you know the wind direction, you can deduce from this which tack and approximate point of sail the other vessel is on, figure out who is privileged and who is burdened, and take appropriate action (keeping in mind, of course, that the other vessel may or may not have seen and interpreted your running lights correctly and may or may not be relied upon to take appropriate action).

A motorboat, *which includes any sailboat with its auxiliary motor operating*, must, in addition to the basic configuration, show a 20-point white "steaming" light (also known as *bow light*) visible above both the red and green port and starboard lights. So if you're sailing at night and decide to start your engine, you must also turn on your steaming light (Figure 5.9).

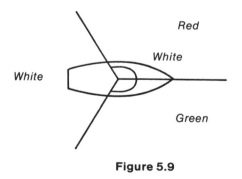

Figure 5.9

In the case of motorboats, the boat on the right is privileged and should hold its course and speed. The boat on the left is burdened and should alter course, slow down, or stop to avoid collision. Note that the privileged boat looks at the burdened boat and sees a green light (white light above), while the burdened boat looks at the privileged boat and sees a red light (white light above). From this came our automobile traffic lights (Figure 5.10).

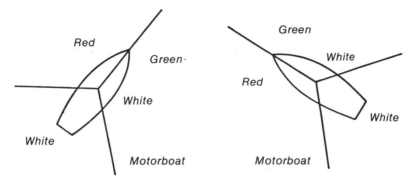

Figure 5.10

We have discussed running light requirements on sailboats and small motorboats. Bear in mind, however, that there are perhaps 30 different running light combinations we have not discussed that are used to differentiate among pilot boats, fishing boats (the lights vary depending on what method they use to catch fish!), tugs pushing, tugs pulling, barges, vessels over 50 meters in length, vessels anchored, vessels aground, vessels restricted by their draft, dredges, etc., to mention a few. Further, requirements for running lights vary somewhat between *Inland* (domestic) and *International Rules of the Road.*

Before sailing at night, it is a good idea to learn thoroughly the running light conventions for different types of boats, both to ensure that your boat is properly lit and to help in interpreting the lights of other vessels.

Keep in mind, too, that if you see a single white light, for example, while sailing at night, it could be the stern light of another boat or a guy in a rowboat with a flashlight, but it could also be a motorcycle, a street light, or any number of other things. Constant vigilance and continuous re-evaluation of input are essential for safe night sailing.

6

TIDES AND CURRENTS

In most bodies of water with a direct link to the ocean, the water level rises and falls once, or more commonly twice a day. This phenomenon is called a *tide*. The highest water level reached in a given tide cycle is called *high tide*; the lowest, *low tide*.

Tide refers to the vertical rise and fall of the level of the sea due to gravitational effects of the moon and the sun. The difference in water level between high tide and low tide is called the *tidal range*. Since the actual heights of high tide and low tide in a given location vary (for reasons we shall discuss later), we speak of *mean high tide* (also called *mean high water*) and *mean low tide* (*mean low water*) as the average high and low tides in a given location. *Mean tidal range* is the difference in height between mean high and mean low waters. In Boston Harbor, for example, the mean tidal range is 10 feet.

Note: On most charts, water depths are indicated at mean low water.

In coastal inlets, harbors, and rivers, the tide level rises as water flows in from the ocean (*floods*). As the tide level drops, water generally flows back out (*ebbs*). This horizontal flow of water is known as *tidal current*. In some locations, maximum tidal current can flow at speeds of up to several knots.

In most bays and harbors that have a relatively wide opening to the sea, the relationship between tide and current is this: The current floods until high tide, at which time the current stops flooding and is said to be at *slack water prior to ebb*. The current then begins to ebb and the tide drops until *slack water prior to flood*, and so on. Please note that this idealized relationship between tides and currents does not apply everywhere and in fact in some places behaves nothing like this. You must check tide tables and tidal current tables for accurate information in the area where you sail.

Knowing the exact state of the tide and current is a matter of more than academic interest to anyone who operates a boat in tidal waters. For instance, some harbor entrances are too shallow to use at or near low tide. Some bridges are too low to pass under at high tide.

Note: On most charts, bridge clearances are indicated above mean high water.

Also, when you suddenly find yourself faced with the unfortunate reality of having run aground, the first thing you should think about (after you calm down) is the exact state of the tide. In locations where the current reaches speeds of half a knot or more, you generally want to plan your daysailing so that the current goes with you when you return in the evening—especially if you don't have a motor and you're sailing in a seabreeze, which typically dies in the evening. Otherwise, bring running lights and provisions.

Another time to consider tides is when anchoring or mooring your boat. If you anchor in 10 feet of water at high tide and the tide range is 10 feet, you are not going to like low tide! And it is essential to know the state of the tide if you are going to tie your boat to a nonfloating pier and leave it for a while. Possibly the most embarrassing thing you can do is to tie your boat to a nonfloating pier at high tide and come back several hours later to find it hanging there, dock lines stretched to about two octaves above middle C.

All in all, tides are important enough that we should look more closely at how they work. The moon is the principal body responsible for earth tides. However, its gravitational attraction is not equal everywhere on earth because gravity works on the "inverse square law," which states that although one side of the earth is only slightly closer to the moon than the other side, the moon pulls substantially harder on the closer side (Figure 6.1).

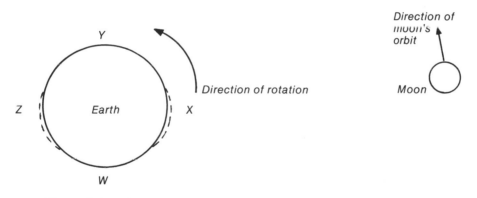

Figure 6.1   *Moon's gravitational effects cause high tide bulges at X and Z.*

In the situation shown in Figure 6.1, the moon pulls harder on point "X" than on the center of the earth, resulting in a bulge at point "X," and it pulls harder on the center of the earth than on point "Z," resulting in a bulge at point "Z." So at "X" and "Z" it is high tide. At "Y" and "W" it is low tide. Notice that as the earth rotates you pass through "X," "Y," "Z," and "W," or high, low, high, low, at six-hour intervals. After 24 hours, when you are back at "X," the moon has traveled about another one-twenty-eighth of its orbit, so high tide occurs roughly 50 minutes later each day.

This simplified explanation does not take into account land masses (which impede the advance of this "tidal wave") or local topographical conditions, which combine to help create variations such as a 35-foot mean tidal range in parts of Nova

Scotia as compared with a negligible tide in the Bahamas and parts of Scandinavia.

Two factors that affect the tidal range on a daily basis, however, are the phase of the moon and the distance of the moon from the earth (see Figure 6.2).

The sun, which is much farther from the earth than the moon is, has a lesser effect on tides. It does exert some influence, however, so that when the moon is full or new and the sun and moon line up with the earth, their tidal effects combine to create more extreme tides—higher highs and lower lows. These extreme conditions are called *spring tides* (which have nothing to do with the season of the same name), and they occur twice per month.

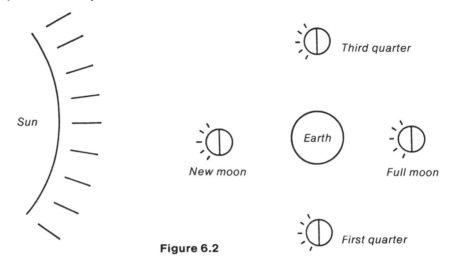

Figure 6.2

When the moon is in its first or third quarter, the tidal effect of the sun reduces that of the moon, resulting in tides that are less extreme than average. These are called *neap tides*.

In addition to the phase of the moon, its distance from the earth affects the range of tide on a given day, too. The moon's orbit about the earth is elliptical. When the moon is as close to the earth as it gets (*perigee*), tides are more extreme than average. When the moon is at *apogee* (the farthest away that it gets), tides are less extreme.

It is now apparent that, as a result of the moon's phase and its distance from earth (as well as events such as severe storms), the heights of high and low tides vary day to day. Some days, low tide can be substantially lower than mean low tide (which is the state of the tide at which water depths are generally indicated on charts). In Boston Harbor, for example, extreme low tide can be as much as 2½ feet below the soundings on the chart. Keep this in mind when you are deciding where to sail your boat.

Accurate information on tides and currents is available from several sources. A few that offer information for the eastern United States are: *Boating Almanac, Waterway Guide, Eldridge,* the National Ocean Survey (NOS) *Tide Tables – East Coast of North and South America*, and NOS *Tidal Current Tables – Atlantic Coast of North America*. Figures 6.3 and 6.4 show how to use these tables.

Figure 6.3   Typical Section from Tide Table

```
          BOSTON, MASS., 1985
 Times and Heights of High and Low Waters

                    MAY

      Time    Height        Time    Height
 Day                    Day
      h m    ft    m         h m    ft    m

  1  0139   0.3   0.1    16  0248   0.8   0.2
  W  0748   9.9   3.0    Th  0858   8.7   2.7
     1407  -0.4  -0.1        1501   0.9   0.3
     2020  10.1   3.1        2116   9.3   2.8

  2  0234  -0.5  -0.2    17  0330   0.5   0.2
  Th 0845  10.3   3.1    F   0941   8.8   2.7
     1458  -0.8  -0.2        1540   0.8   0.2
     2111  10.8   3.3        2154   9.5   2.9
```

Tide tables work like this: For each day of the year, we're shown the times (Eastern Standard Time—add one hour for Daylight Savings Time) of high and low tide and the height above or below mean low water in feet and meters (mean low is 0.0 feet).

Note that on Wednesday, May 1, 1985, high tide, which was 9.9 feet above the soundings on the chart, occurred at 8:48 a.m. At 3:07 p.m., there was a low tide .4 feet below the soundings on the chart. Note that we automatically add an hour to the indicated time in any month when we are on Daylight Savings Time.

Figure 6.4   Typical Section from Tidal Current Table

Tidal current tables work like this: For each day of the year, we're shown the times of slack water, the time of the next maximum current, the velocity (in knots) of that maximum current, and whether it is a flood or ebb current. The direction of flood and ebb is indicated at the top of the page.

```
 BOSTON HARBOR (Deer Island Light), MASSACHUSETTS, 1985

   F-Flood, Dir. 254° True    E-Ebb, Dir. 111° True

                       MAY

      Slack   Maximum           Slack   Maximum
      Water   Current           Water   Current
      Time    Time  Vel.        Time    Time  Vel.
 Day                       Day
      h.m.    h.m.  knots        h.m.    h.m.  knots

  1   0139    0430  1.2F    16           0024  1.3E
  W   0723    1122  1.3E    Th   0247    0601  1.0F
      1405    1708  1.3F         0843    1246  1.2E
      1956    2356  1.3E         1501    1822  1.1F
                                 2107

  2   0233    0535  1.3F    17           0111  1.3E
  Th  0819    1213  1.4E    F    0331    0646  1.1F
      1456    1801  1.5F         0924    1331  1.2E
      2049                       1543    1905  1.2F
                                 2141
```

So on May 1, 1985, in Boston Harbor the current is slack at 2:39 a.m. It then begins to flood (see the "F" at the end of that row?), accelerating to its maximum velocity of 1.2 knots, which it reaches at 5:30 a.m., and then slowing until the next slack water is reached at 8:23 a.m.

If you compare this information with the information from the tide table, you see that in Boston Harbor high tide and slack water prior to ebb current occur within 25 minutes of each other. This close correlation occurs in many places but by no means all.

7

ANCHORING

It is important to master the skill of anchoring properly because it is possible to get in trouble as a result of anchoring improperly.

Figure 7.1 shows the types of anchors in most common use today. Of these, the *danforth* type is the most versatile. It provides the greatest holding power for the least weight. Most cruising boats in the 30-foot range carry two danforths, a 12-pounder and a 20-pounder, for example. They are made of either steel or high-tensile steel, which is more effective because the points stay sharper and penetrate better. Several companies manufacture danforth-type anchors. They all work, *except* for the shiny, vinyl-coated kind designed not to mar your deck. Unfortunately, vinyl-coated points do not penetrate anything harder than soft mud.

The uncoated danforth anchor works well on almost any bottom. The only conditions under which it won't hold is when the bottom is infested with weeds. Even then, several tries may get the anchor down to good holding ground.

The *CQR* (British code for "secure") or *plow* anchor is slightly more reliable on weedy bottoms, and boats set up for extended cruising usually carry a plow as well as a danforth or two.

The *yachtsman* anchor has small flukes so it has to be big and heavy to be effective, but a 60- or 100-pound yachtsman will hold in weed or gravel or anything. Boats 40 feet and larger equipped for long-range cruising should have one of these on board.

The *claw* anchor has the commendable feature of folding up into a compact shape for storage. Unfortunately, it cannot be relied upon to hold a boat under any conditions.

Since the danforth is the most common type of anchor, our discussion will focus on it. It works on the same principle as other types of anchors (Figure 7.2): If the anchor is lying on the bottom and a force pulls more or less parallel to the bottom, the flukes will dig in. The harder the pull, the more they dig in. But the force must be parallel to the bottom or the anchor will lift instead of dig in. There are two things you

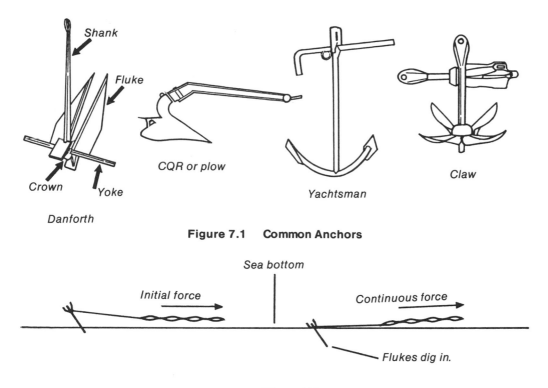

Shank

Fluke

Crown

Yoke

Danforth

CQR or plow

Yachtsman

Claw

Figure 7.1   Common Anchors

Sea bottom

Initial force

Continuous force

Flukes dig in.

Figure 7.2

can do to ensure that the force pulling on the anchor shank will be approximately parallel to the bottom:

1. Incorporate a section of chain into the anchor end of the *rode* (anchor line) so the weight of the chain holds that end down. The anchor end of the rode is also the most likely to chafe against stones, etc., on the bottom, which is another point in favor of a length of chain.
2. Pay out enough *scope* (the ratio of anchor rode to depth of the water) so the rode makes a very shallow angle at the anchor. A scope of 4 to 1 is minimum for safety; 7 to 1 is much better. So if you anchor in 10 feet of water, you should let out at least 40 feet of rode (Figure 7.3).

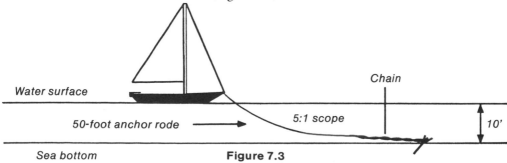

Water surface

Chain

50-foot anchor rode

5:1 scope

10'

Sea bottom   **Figure 7.3**

When choosing a place to anchor, look for a place that is sheltered from the wind and waves and offers the boat room to swing around the anchor if the wind or current changes direction. Also, if you anchor at high tide, check the tide tables to be sure you won't be aground when the tide goes out, and if you happen to anchor at low tide, you must take the tidal range into account when paying out your scope. For example, if you were to anchor in 10 feet of water with a 5-to-1 scope—50 feet—at low tide but there was a 12-foot tidal range, then at high tide your 50 feet of scope will be not 5 to 1 but just over 2 to 1! Remember you're now resting in 22 feet of water with inadequate scope. If the wind pipes up—as it often can—then you will drag your anchor: not fun. The point is, know the state of the tide when anchoring.

It is good practice, before lowering the anchor, to be sure that the *bitter end* of the anchor rode (the end that is not secured to the anchor) is secured to some solid part of the boat, just in case. I had a friend once who sailed in the Niagara River about six miles above the falls. He was motoring one evening when the engine died. He lowered his anchor, being careful to pay out enough scope to hold against the powerful, three-knot current running towards the falls, when the bitter end slipped through his fingers. Alas.

So before you lower the anchor, secure the bitter end. Also, be sure the rode is properly coiled so it runs out freely.

Then head into the wind in the place you want to anchor and, when the boat comes to a stop, carefully lower the anchor. As the boat drifts backward, pay out scope. When you've got enough scope, tug the rode hard to feel if it is set. When it is, cleat it. Line up a couple of landmarks to orient yourself and, before you retire for the night or head for shore, check your landmarks again to be sure you're not drifting.

Weighing anchor (getting it up) is not usually difficult. You either pull the boat along the rode or motor, gathering in the rode as you go until you are directly over the anchor. A good tug then usually breaks it free.

Sometimes, though, the flukes will be caught on some undersea obstruction and the anchor will be stuck. What do you do? Anchors are expensive, so cutting the line is not the best solution. Here are some methods that work for raising a stuck anchor.

1. Try pulling the rode from different directions. This sometimes loosens the anchor.
2. Motor or sail towards the anchor, gathering in the rode, so that you still have some *way on* (speed) when you reach the point directly over the anchor. Then *snub* the rode around the bow cleat (wrap it around a couple of times and hold tension on it) and let the momentum of the boat break the anchor free. This usually works. Note: It can be quite embarrassing if you forget to snub the rode around the cleat.
3. Use a jib winch to get it up. In fact, a winch generates so much power that one technique for refloating a boat that has run aground is to set an anchor in deep water and winch the boat up to the anchor.

4. Use a *trip line*. A trip line is a light line attached to the crown of the anchor at one end and a floating buoy at the other end. When you are ready to weigh anchor, merely pull the trip line, and the anchor comes out the way it went it. If you use one, this always works (Figure 7.4). Unfortunately, *trip line* is most commonly used in the expression, "We should have had a trip line."

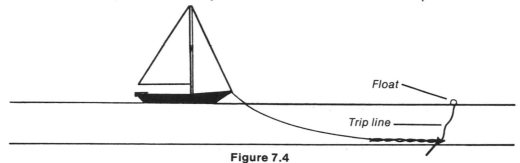

Figure 7.4

These are the measures with which I have had the most success raising stuck anchors. There are others, and when you begin cruising extensively you will undoubtedly have opportunities to exercise your imagination along these lines.

8

BASICS OF NAVIGATION

Navigation is the art of staying out of trouble.

The most important tool of the navigator by far is the chart, without which it is virtually impossible to navigate successfully.

One of the most important pieces of information on the chart is the date, usually located in the lower left corner (Figure 8.1). This tells you how accurate you can reasonably expect the information on the chart to be. New charts in most high-population areas come out on the order of every year; however, you can keep your local charts as current as possible by subscribing to *Local Notices to Mariners*, a weekly publication that the U.S. Coast Guard will happily send you if you call and request it (you've already paid for it).

Another important piece of information is located in the legend, where the units of depth as well as the state of the tide to which they refer are indicated. Most local area U.S. charts are *sounded* in feet at mean low water. Some charts, however, are sounded in meters or fathoms (1 fathom = 6 feet), and some charts are sounded at extreme low water (Figure 8.2).

U.S. charts are generally printed in four colors: yellow for land, white for deep water, blue for shallower water, and green for marsh—territory that is above water at low tide but submerged at high tide.

On the Boston Harbor chart, the numbers on the water areas refer to the depth of the water in feet at mean low tide. On that particular chart the blue shaded water is 18 feet deep or less; white water is deeper than 18 feet. Note: Boston Inner Harbor is shaded blue not because it is 18 feet or less but because NOS feels that the scale of this chart is not adequate to show sufficient detail in the Inner Harbor area and that you should get chart #13272 to navigate there.

The asterisks in many of the shallow areas stand for rocks. From this information you can see that you do not want to sail where the asterisks are, nor do you want to sail where the depth of the water is equal to or less than the draft of your boat. Keep in mind that extreme low tide (in Boston) can be as much as 2½ feet lower than mean

47th Ed., Nov. 20/82 ■

13270

Figure 8.1

BOSTON HARBOR

Mercator Projection
Scale 1:25,000 at Lat. 42°19′
North American 1927 Datum

SOUNDINGS IN FEET
AT MEAN LOW WATER

Figure 8.2

U.S. charts are produced by the National Ocean Survey (NOS) of the U.S. Department of Commerce. They are readily availble at marine chandleries. You can also pick up for free the NOS chart catalog to determine which charts you will need for the area in which you plan to sail. In 1985 NOS charts cost about $5.50 each. However, Waterway Guide and Better Boating Association both publish chart books, which offer numerous charts covering large geographical areas for $32 to $55 per book. These books are also more compact than NOS charts and fit on chart tables of small cruising sailboats.

---

low, and that a boat with 5-foot draft in 7 feet of water will touch bottom hard if there are 3-foot waves. Therefore, in most cases, the prudent navigator will allow a bit extra water than his boat draws.

The key to successful navigation is to navigate *continuously*, that is, always be able to determine the position of your boat on the chart and continuously anticipate from information on the chart what you should expect to see next. In order to do this, you need to be able to match various objects that you see from your boat with their corresponding symbols on the chart. Initially, it may be helpful when looking at a chart to imagine your eyeball right down on the chart, looking radially along the surface of the paper just as you look along the surface of the water from your boat.

LANDMARKS AND AIDS TO NAVIGATION

The kinds of items that help relate what you see from your boat to information on the chart are classified as *landmarks* and *aids to navigation*. Useful landmarks are things like cities or towns, airports, standpipes (large, cylindrical storage containers), stacks, radio towers, water towers, other kinds of towers, piers along the shoreline, hills or land formations (as indicated by contour lines), bluffs (as indicated by a series of hash marks along a shore), buildings, cupolas, etc.

Aids to navigation are installed and maintained by the Coast Guard specifically to help you relate what you see to the appropriate symbols on the chart. Aids to navigation are of two types, *fixed* and *floating*. Fixed aids to navigation consist of *beacons*, which, curiously enough, are not lighted, and *lighthouses*, which are.

Beacons are generally placed right on a shoal or a rock, so you should never cruise up to one to check it out. Usually, a beacon will consist of either a red triangle or a

Figure 8.3a

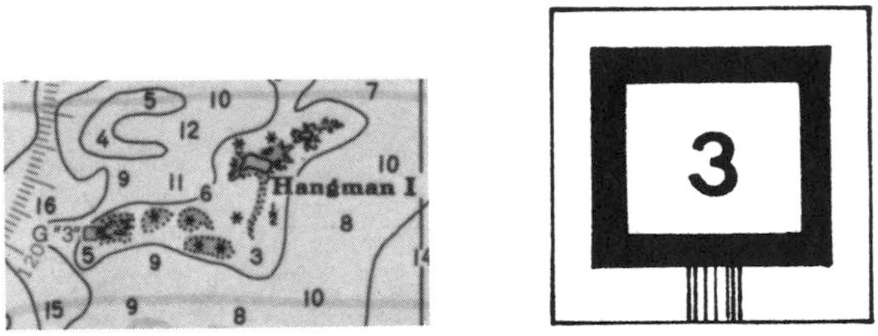

Figure 8.3b

Figure 8.3c

green or black square mounted on a post. The respective chart symbols will be a red triangle, a green square or black triangle, usually with the letters "Bn." The color differences are mainly to conform to channel marking conventions, which we will discuss later. In any case, knowing the color scheme is much less important than being able to match an aid to navigation with its symbol on the chart and determine which side (if any) of the aid you want to be on (Figures 8.3a to 8.3c).

Occasionally, a beacon will not quite conform to the above description but will be denoted on the chart by a triangle and the letters "Bn" (Figure 8.4).

Nixes Mate Beacon.
BWBn = black and white beacon

Figure 8.4

Lighthouses are distinguished from beacons by the fact that they are lighted at night. Each lighthouse has its own *characteristic* (light color and flash pattern), which is noted on the chart along with other valuable information about the lighthouse. A lighthouse is symbolized on the chart by a red (officially magenta) exclamation point. The dot represents the exact location of the lighthouse. Let's look at some examples (Figures 8.5 to 8.11):

Floating aids to navigation, or *buoys*, are primarily used to mark channels. They are held in place by an anchor and chain and are considered marginally less reliable than fixed aids to navigation. They can be seen from a maximum distance of one to two miles from a sailboat.

F1 G 4sec 15ft 5M "5" Horn

Figure 8.5

Figure 8.5 *This tells us that the lighthouse shows a green flash once every four seconds, that the light is 15 feet above mean high tide, that it plays a horn in low visibility conditions such as fog, that on a clear night you might expect to be able to see the light from a maximum distance of about five miles, and that it also happens to play the role of Marker "5" in a channel numbering system (we'll get to that later).*

Boston Light - Fl 10sec 102ft 27M Horn

Figure 8.6 *Boston Light shows a single white flash (when no other color is indicated the light is white) every 10 seconds. How high is the light above mean high tide? How far away might you reasonably expect to see it? What does it do in fog?*

Figure 8.7 *"F" stands for "fixed"— it's always on. Since no other color is indicated, the light is white.*

Long Island Head Light - F 120ft 9M

Figure 8.8 *"Gp" stands for "group"—a group of white flashes (two, to be exact) that repeats every 12 seconds.*

Graves Light - Gp Fl(2) 12sec 98ft 24M Horn

Figure 8.9 *"Qk Fl" means "quick flashing," which indicates that the light flashes about once every second. In this case, the light flashes green.*

Windmill Point Light - Qk Fl G 20ft 5M "3"

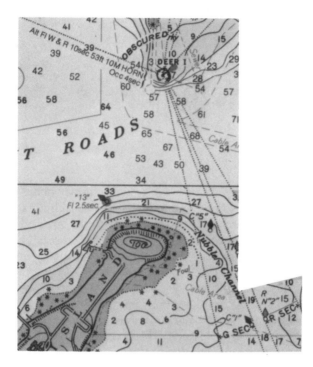

Deer Island Light - Alt F1 W & R 10sec 53ft
10M Horn
Occ 4sec

Figure 8.10 *"Alt F1 W & R 10sec" ("alternating flashing white and red") is the principal characteristic of Deer Island Light—a white flash followed by a red flash, with the cycle repeating every 10 seconds.*

But the chart indicates that the lighthouse also shows another characteristic: "Occ 4sec." "Occ" stands for "occulting" and refers to a light that is normally on but briefly flashes off, in this case, once every four seconds. What is interesting about this occulting light, however, is that it does not refer to the main light, but to a separate light that is divided into green, white, and red sectors that radiate south/southeast towards Nubble Channel. When the occulting light appears white from your boat, you are safely in the channel, but when it appears green or red, you are respectively west or east of the channel and should immediately remedy that situation.

One more thing about this light: See the squiggly circle around the dot that stands for the exact position of the light? The squiggly circle stands for riprap. Riprap is a pile of very large rocks placed around some lighthouses to protect them from boats.

Figure 8.11 *"E Int" stands for "equal interval" and means that the period of "light on" equals the period of "light off"; in this case, three seconds each, since the cycle repeats every six seconds. What color is the light?*

E Int R 6sec 25ft

Most channel marking buoys are red or black (slowly being replaced by green), and they are conventionally used to mark channels in such a way that as you return towards harbor from the sea, red buoys will be on your right and black buoys will be on your left if you are in the channel. As you head out to sea, black buoys will be on your right, red ones on your left. Remember the famous mnemonic device: "*Red Right Returning*"; "*Black Right Out*" works, too.

(It should be pointed out, however, that in 1982 the Coast Guard, in order to conform to international convention, began painting black buoys green, changing red and black junction markers to red and green, and changing white and black midchannel markers to white and red. The corresponding chart symbols are being altered to reflect these changes. The project is not scheduled to be completed before 1989, so, to avoid confusion, this text will refer to the buoy system still predominantly in use in U.S. waters.)

Red buoys and black buoys are always numbered: Red buoys are even numbered, black buoys odd numbered. They are numbered in order, starting from the seaward end of the channel, so that, as you enter a channel from seaward, you first encounter Red Buoy "2" on your right and/or Black Buoy "1" on your left. The numbers increase as you proceed toward the harbor.

Buoys are symbolized on the chart by a diamond (red for a red buoy and black for a black buoy) with a large dot at one of the points. The dot indicates the position of the buoy. The number of the buoy is indicated next to the diamond and is always in quotes so that it cannot be confused with the depth of the water.

If the buoy is lighted, there will be a circle around the dot and the color and characteristic of the light will be indicated nearby. A red light seen at night will only be used on a red buoy (or other aid to navigation designed to mark the right side of a channel to a vessel returning); a green light seen at night will only be used on a black buoy (or an aid to navigation marking the left side of a channel to a vessel returning). A white light may be used for either application.

Whether lighted or unlighted, buoys may be equipped with a sound-making device (such as a bell, gong, whistle, diaphone, horn, etc.). If so, this information will also appear on the chart near the symbol for the buoy.

Let's look at some examples of chart symbols for buoys (Figures 8.12 to 8.16).

Nun "2"

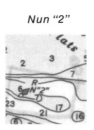

Figure 8.12 *An unlighted red buoy equipped with no sound device will usually be a nun.*

Can "3"

Figure 8.13 *An unlighted black buoy equipped with no sound device will usually be a can.*

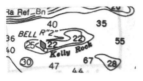

Figure 8.14 *Red Bell "2" (unlighted). The plates that form the top of the buoy are constructed to form right-angled corners to reflect radar effectively. Sometimes the letters "Ra Ref" (radar reflector) will appear on the chart to indicate this fact.*

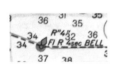

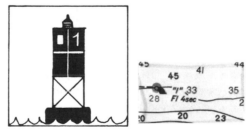

Figure 8.15 *Red Bell "4" (lighted— a flashing red light every four second)*

Figure 8.16 *Black Buoy "1" (lighted—a flashing white light every four seconds)*

Cans, nuns, or other unlighted buoys usually have a band of reflective paint so that they show up in the beam of a searchlight at night.

Variations on the above described red and black buoys are used to mark the edges of both big ship channels and small boat channels (for example, Figure 8.17).

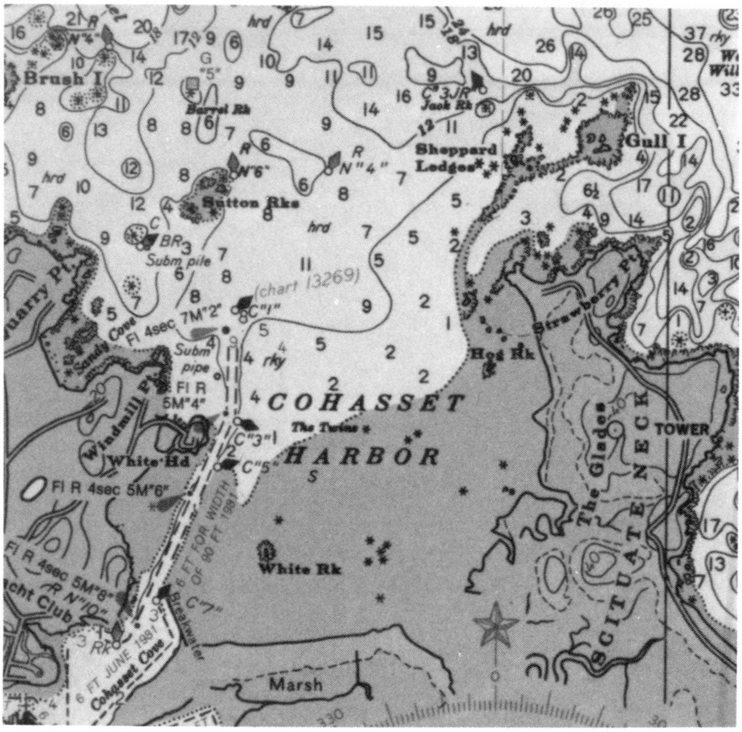

Figure 8.17

Examine the entrance channel into Cohasset Cove: The black cans will be on your left (entering), odd numbered beginning with Can "1" and ending with Can "7." This channel uses lighthouse structures to mark its right side, even numbered beginning with Nun "2" and ending with Nun "10." The chart reveals that you could not take any boat even slightly outside the channel without running aground. Compare this with President Roads, the entrance channel into Boston Inner Harbor. This channel is made for big ships, and in a small boat (under, say, 100 feet), there is no reason to restrict yourself to the main ship channel, as long as you avoid Lower Middle Shoal and Governors Island Flats. However, you can do this safely only by continuously referring to your chart.

In fact, notwithstanding any channel marking conventions, the prudent navigator always consults the chart, locates the symbols for the approaching aids to navigation, and from the chart determines where to steer relative to the aids to navigation in question.

For example, find Nubble Channel on the chart on page 101. Just looking at it, can you tell which way is returning and which way is heading to seaward? Closer examination reveals that, heading northward through the channel, you will be in deep water (15 feet) if you keep the nuns to your right and the cans to your left. So the Coast Guard set up the channel as if heading north were returning (note also that the buoy numbers increase going northward). Fine, but in the case of Nubble Channel, this is a somewhat arbitrary decision. In another place, the exact same buoy configuration is used to indicate that there are two channels: a west channel where one heads to seaward with the black cans "close aboard" to the right, an east channel where one heads to seaward with the red nuns close aboard on the left, and shoal water between the two channels.

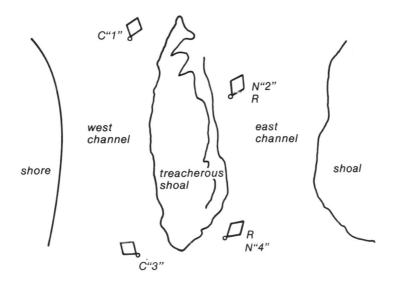

Figure 8.18 *A possible alternative meaning for a buoy configuration like that in Nubble Channel. Your chart tells you where the good water is.*

In addition to red buoys and black buoys, which are used mainly to mark the edges of channels, there are two other types of floating navigational aids in common use: *junction* or *obstruction* markers, and *midchannel* markers.

A junction marker is used to mark a shoal, rock, or island that you should pass to one side or the other. The marker is located at the junction of two possible channels around the obstruction. (See Figures 8.19 to 8.21).

Junction markers are not numbered. Rather, such a marker is symbolized on the chart by a diamond, half red and half black, and the notation "RB" or "BR." The buoy itself shows alternating horizontal red and black bands (slowly being replaced with red and green). When lighted, a junction marker generally shows the characteristic "*I Qk Fl*" or "interrupted quick flash" (i.e., quick flashing for a few seconds, then off for a few seconds, etc.).

The color of the top band and the shape (i.e., can or nun) indicate which of the two

Figure 8.19 *This lighted junction buoy is placed to mark a 21-foot-deep shoal, which is of no concern to the small boat navigator but could matter to a ship.*

Figure 8.20 *This junction buoy marks Outer Seal Rock. The buoy is a can, so the top band is black.*

Figure 8.21 *This buoy marks a shoal that is exposed at low water but submerged at high water. It is a nun, so the top band is red.*

channels is favored in this manner: If you treat the buoy as if it were entirely the color of the top band (which would be consistent with the shape), you would then be taking the favored channel. For example (Figure 8.22).

A midchannel marker is most commonly used to mark the beginning of a major channel. Such markers usually occur to seaward of Black Buoy "1" and Red "2," and are therefore frequently referred to as *sea buoys*. They are painted with alternating vertical black and white stripes (being slowly changed to red and white) and are symbolized on the chart by a clear diamond with a line down the long axis and the letters "BW." They are not numbered, but they have identifying letters—usually the initials of the channel that they mark. They are usually lighted with the characteristic "Mo(A)," which stands for Morse code letter "A," or a short flash followed by a long flash (Figure 8.23).

In addition to red buoys, black buoys, junction buoys, and midchannel buoys, there are *buoys of special application*, used to mark things like fishing areas, torpedo ranges, quarantine areas, regatta sites, etc. They are symbolized by diamonds that are easily distinguishable from those used for the more common navigational aids. In many cases, the chart shows a notation that indicates their purpose (Figure 8.24).

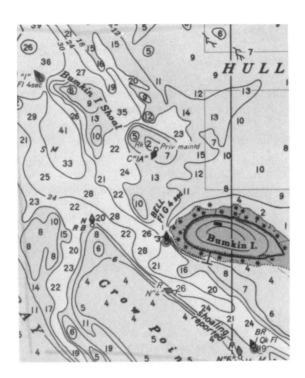

Figure 8.22

This junction marker indicates that if you are coming from the north, you should go around Crow Point Flats either to the east or the west. Reasonable, since Crow Point Flats is a 4-foot shoal. Now from the chart we know that this buoy is a nun (see the "N" near the "RB"?), and therefore, the top band will be red, consistent with the fact that it is a nun, and the favored channel can be found by treating it as a red buoy. That is, since you are returning towards harbor, keep it to your right. The eastern channel is favored because it is deeper and better marked than the western channel.

Note, however, that this arcane convention works only if you are coming from exactly the right direction; the information about which channel is bigger or deeper is readily available by looking at the chart; and which channel is favored as far as you're concerned depends mainly on which way you want to go.

But the real value of this buoy and its symbol on the chart is this: Suppose you are sailing out of the channel between Crow Point Flats and Bumkin Island. Like all good navigators, you are scanning your chart ahead of your present position in anticipation of buoys and other significant things. Your chart tells you that you should expect to see a junction buoy (which happens to be a nun) to the west of Black Bell "3" off Bumkin Island, and if you keep this buoy to your left, then you are definitely in good water. Get it?

Figure 8.23   *Midchannel marker "NC" with the typical characteristic Mo(A). This one also has a gong.*

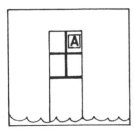

Figure 8.24   *White Gong "A" is a buoy of special application. Along with three other white buoys, it marks an anchorage for ships. On the Boston Harbor chart on page 101, one buoy appears just to the west of Deer Island.*

DEAD RECKONING

When you have thoroughly assimilated the above information, you know enough to "eyeball"-navigate your way around most harbors and coastal areas in clear weather. *Eyeball navigation* describes situations in which you can always see your next navigational aid. Alas, the weather is not always clear, and sometimes we wish to sail farther than we can see. Luckily, we have the *compass* and a technique called *dead reckoning*, which is the basis of all modern coastal and offshore navigation.

The compass, by aligning itself with the earth's magnetic field, indicates *magnetic north* and 360° clockwise around. East is 90°, south is 180°, west is 270°, and north is 0° or 360°. Using a compass, you can steer an accurate course without other reference points. (Please note that this and the following discussion of the principles of dead reckoning assume no currents. In some areas, this would be a rash assumption.)

Dead reckoning (which comes, interestingly enough, from the naval abbreviation for *deduced reckoning*, or *ded. reckoning*) is based on the principle that if you sail a compass course from a known starting point and know your speed to some degree of accuracy, then you can use the formula

$$\text{speed} \times \text{time} = \text{distance}$$

to compute how far you have traveled along your course line at any time, provided that you noted the time when you were at the known starting point. If you plot courses from buoy to buoy or buoy to lighthouse, etc., then each such aid to navigation that you use as a turning point becomes a new known starting point. You navigate by steering a series of such course lines, writing down the time at each turning buoy. By so doing, you can pinpoint your *dead reckoning position* (DR) on the chart at any instant.

Inherent in the philosophy of dead reckoning is recognition of the fact that the farther you travel a given course line, the less accurate your DR is likely to be as a result of compass error, helmsman error, inaccuracy in your speed estimate, or currents that you may not have taken into consideration, etc. We therefore need techniques to redetermine our position when we are in open water or between navigational aids.

Let's examine this situation more closely. If you look at the chart on page 000, or any other chart that you're particularly fond of, you will find one or more *compass roses*. Each rose consists of two circles: an outer circle that points to *true north* and 360° clockwise around and an inner circle that points to *magnetic north* and 360° clockwise around. The difference between true and magnetic direction is called *variation*, which in Boston is about 15 degrees and changes each year by an insignificant amount. The amount of variation depends on your location, but for most places it does not change significantly over the distance you can sail in a day; so, for purposes of small boat coastal navigation, you can forget about true courses and stick with the inner or magnetic circle for plotting magnetic courses and bearings. This eliminates considerations of variation and therefore reduces the possibility of error.

There is one type of compass error that must be considered, though, and it's called *deviation*. Deviation is the effect on the compass of your boat's magnetic field. Your anchor, inboard or outboard motor, steel icebox, radio, and other electronic equipment combine to create a magnetic field that can cause your compass to "lie." Also, the amount of deviation will vary, depending on your compass heading. Fortunately, it is possible to adjust the better compasses by means of internal magnets to eliminate almost totally the effects of deviation on a sailboat. So if you spend $60,000 for a sailboat and $250 for a good compass, hire a professional compass adjuster for $150 to come and *swing* your compass to eliminate deviation. Or get a book on the subject and swing your own compass (either way, do it *after* all your electronics, motor, anchor, etc., are in their permanent locations).

Once we know that our compass will tell us the actual magnetic heading of the boat, we can plot a magnetic course from one known point to another and have a reasonable expectation of being able to sail that course line accurately. There are numerous techniques for plotting a course. Let's look at a technique using *parallel rules* (Figures 8.25 and 8.26).

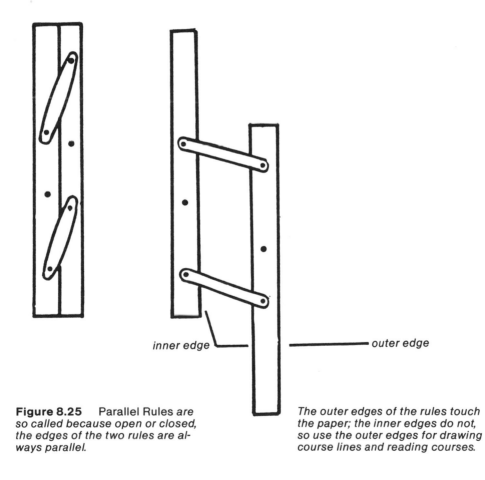

inner edge ⌐ outer edge

Figure 8.25 Parallel Rules are so called because open or closed, the edges of the two rules are always parallel.

The outer edges of the rules touch the paper; the inner edges do not, so use the outer edges for drawing course lines and reading courses.

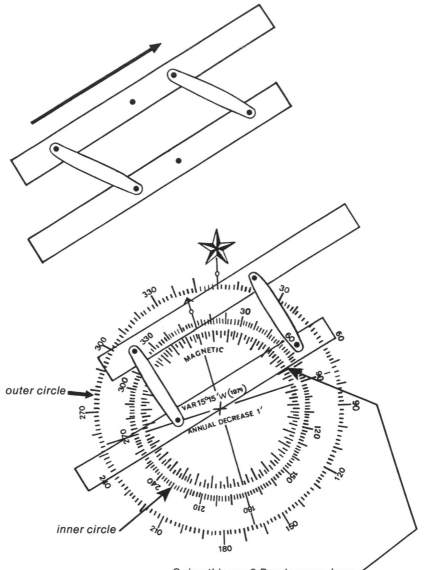

outer circle ➡

inner circle

Going this way? Read course here.

Figure 8.26 *To plot a course from Buoy "11" to Buoy "7," place the outer edge of one of the rules on the dots that represent the actual position of the two buoys. Lightly draw that line in pencil. Then, being careful not to slip, "walk" the rules to the nearest compass rose until one of the outer edges rests exactly on the cross in the center of the rose. Read your compass course on the inner circle in the direction in which you want to go. Write the compass course along the course line you drew between the two buoys with an arrow indicating your direction.*

So if you're at Buoy "11" and you steer 76 degrees, you will arrive at Buoy "7." The logical next question is "when?"

The other important aspect of dead reckoning is measuring distance along a course line. A pair of *dividers* is the right tool for the job. And while charts invariably have at least one scale of miles somewhere in the margins, it is usually easier to use the *latitude* scale (along the sides of the chart) to measure distance. By definition, one nautical mile equals one minute of latitude. A nautical mile is about one-and-one-sixth land or statute miles and is *the* unit of distance in navigation. As mentioned earlier, a knot is one nautical mile per hour (Figure 8.27).

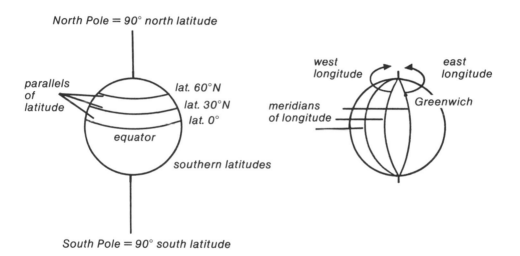

Figure 8.27 **Latitude** *is the distance in degrees measured north or south of the equator through 90 degrees. Since all lines of latitude are parallel to each other, one degree of latitude on the surface of the earth is the same distance no matter where you measure it. Each degree is divided into 60 "minutes"; one nautical mile equals one minute of latitude. On a chart, latitude is indicated along the sides and may be used to measure distance.*

Longitude *is measured in degrees east or west of Greenwich through 180 degrees. (The British controlled the seas when this system was installed.) Notice that the meridians of longitude converge at the poles, so the distance between two adjacent whole degrees of longitude is not consistent. Therefore, the longitude scale may not be used to measure distance. Longitude is indicated along the top and bottom edges of a chart. Note that any point on the earth's surface may be pinpointed using this coordinate system and expressing latitude (north or south) and longitude (east or west) in degrees, minutes, and fractions of minutes. For example, Boston Sailing Center is located at lat. 42° 21.8 N, long. 71° 02.67 W. This is read "Latitude forty two degrees, twenty-one point eight minutes north; longitude seventy-one degrees, two point six seven minutes west."*

To summarize, dead reckoning consists of sailing a series of course lines from one navigational aid to the next (where possible) and noting time of arrival at each navigational aid, so that, knowing your speed, you can find your DR on the chart at any time, within the limits of accuracy of your dead reckoning.

This applies whether you're guessing your speed, estimating your course (as you might reasonably do as a backup to eyeball navigation in, say, an open daysailer with no equipment save chart and compass), or using your "knot-log" for accurate speed and distance and plotting and steering courses accurate to within a degree or two.

FINDING YOUR POSITION

In either case, there are times when it helps to be able to establish your position with some certainty when you are not at a navigational aid (as when you see thick fog suddenly rolling in, or when you're beating and cannot count on being at a navigational aid whenever you tack, to cite but two examples).

The key to locating your position on a chart or getting a "fix" when you are in open water is to establish two or more *lines of position*. Two methods of placing your boat on such lines of position are the use of *ranges* and *bearings*.

Any time two known objects whose symbols appear on the chart line up as seen from your boat, you are on a range. If you draw a straight line through the two symbols on the chart, you know that you are on that line (assuming, of course, that you were correct in matching the symbols with the objects). A range is a fast and accurate method for establishing a line of position. Ranges are so useful that you tend to look for them continuously whenever you sail (Figures 8.28 and 8.29).

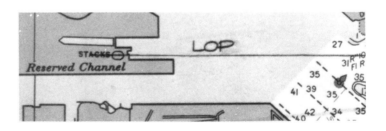

Figure 8.28   Two Examples of Ranges

When these two stacks come into line as seen from your boat, you are exactly on this line of position (LOP). You have to be certain you are looking at the right stacks, of course.

Less accurate but more readily available than a range is a *bearing:* By sighting over your boat's compass or a "hand bearing" compass toward a single known object whose symbol appears on your chart, you determine your compass course, or bearing, toward that object. If you then plot that bearing on the chart so that it passes through

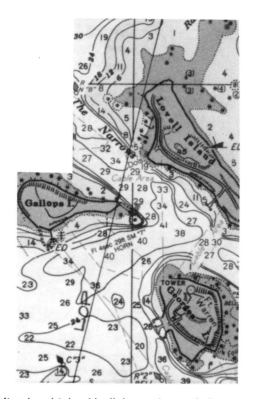

Figure 8.29

A very useful kind of range can often be obtained by lining up tangents to shorelines of land areas. Notice that when you're east of the LOP you can see open water between Gallops and Lovell Islands; west of the LOP you cannot. The beauty of this type of range is that it works even in places that are not well marked, such as the Bahamas.

the object, then that line becomes a line of position; i.e., you are somewhere on that line.

Any time you can cross two or more lines of position on the chart, you have a fix. When deciding among a number of objects on which to take bearings, it is better to choose the closest objects possible for maximum accuracy. It is also desirable to use three lines of position when possible as the size of the triangle obtained where the three lines cross will give you some idea as to the accuracy of your fix. Also, if one of the three objects was not what you thought it was (which will happen on occasion), that fact will be brought graphically to your attention.

Please keep in mind that the above information on dead reckoning and position finding is not meant to be a comprehensive discussion of the subject of navigation. Among the many aspects of navigation that we have not discussed are currents (extremely important in some areas, less so in others) and more sophisticated methods of position finding, including electronic methods. The above discussion is meant only as an introduction, a starting point. The key to learning to navigate successfully, as with most things, is to get out there and do it. Navigate continuously and remember, be careful out there!

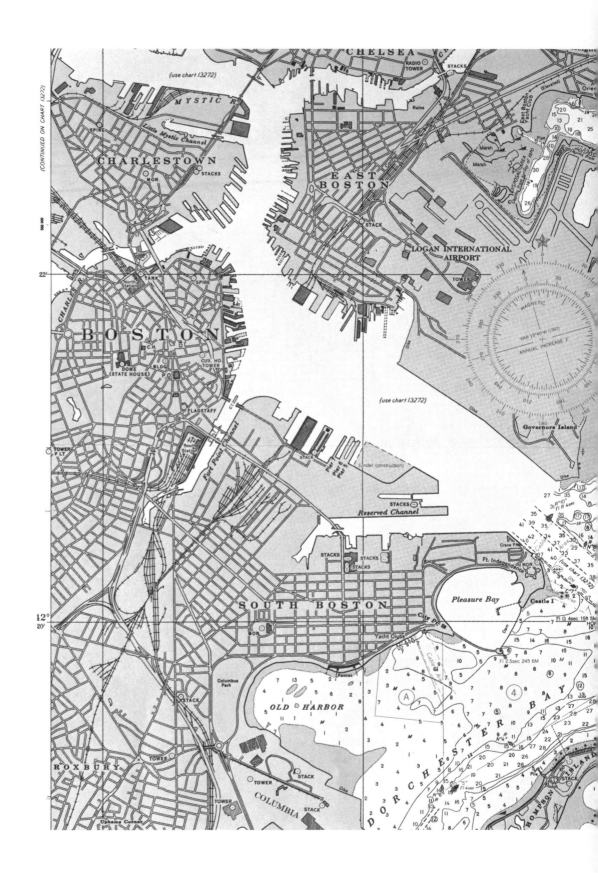

9

SPINNAKER SAILING

Modern boats with their high aspect ratio working sails are designed to sail upwind efficiently, but when they turn downwind and the apparent wind drops off, they do not have much sail area with which to maintain speed. The *spinnaker* or *chute* was designed to increase sail area greatly for downwind sailing.

A modern spinnaker more than doubles your sail area and tremendously increases your downwind speed. (The term *spinnaker* originated in 1866, when the schooner *Sphinx* was seen to be flying what appeared to be an "acre" of sail, which became "Sphinx' acre," or "spinnaker." And while it is mainly a downwind sail to be used on a run, broad reach, or beam reach, a modern, relatively flat spinnaker (or *reacher*) can be used to advantage in light air up to a close reach. Beyond that, it is a beautiful, challenging, and enjoyable sail to use once you have mastered it.

However, there are a few important differences between spinnakers and working sails (mains and jibs). First, you can actually capsize a keel boat with a spinnaker up! You see, unlike the mainsail and jib, which offer progressively smaller projections to the wind as you heel over, the spinnaker just keeps on pulling. So for the first few times you fly a spinnaker, it is a good idea to practice only in light air. Second, you cannot go upwind with a spinnaker up. You must *douse* it first (get it down), which can take some time, especially with a crew that's new to it, so you should only fly it with plenty of good water to leeward. And third, if you are going to fly a chute, someone on board must be prepared to trim it continuously, or, unlike the working sails, it will periodically collapse and refill explosively, making for an unpleasant ride.

We will discuss flying, hoisting, jibing, and dousing the spinnaker, but first, memorize the diagram in Figure 9.1.

To trim the spinnaker, adjust the guy so the pole is at a right angle to the apparent wind (Figure 9.2). On a beam reach the pole will be forward almost against the forestay; on a run it will be back at a right angle to the boat; and on a broad reach it will still be at a right angle to the wind. Once the guy is set, trim the sail with the sheet, as you would trim any sail: Ease the sheet until the luff (windward edge) of the sail

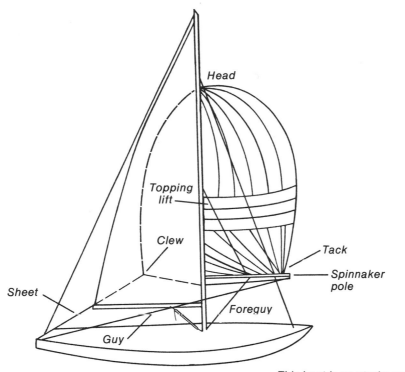

This boat is on starboard tack.

Figure 9.1 *The* spinnaker pole *mounts to windward (opposite the mainsail) with its inboard end secured on a* mast ring. *It is held up by the* topping lift *and held down against the sometimes formidable lifting force of the sail by the* pole downhaul *or* foreguy. *The* guy *passes through the outboard end of the pole and attaches to the* tack *(lower windward corner) of the spinnaker. The* spinnaker sheet *attaches to the* clew *of the sail. The chute is hoisted by a* spinnaker halyard *attached to its* head.

Note: The lines that attach to the two bottom corners of the sail (which generically are called clews) are sheets. But when the sail is flying, the one to windward is the guy and it is attached to the tack. The line to leeward is the sheet, and it is attched to the clew. If you jibe over to the other tack, the pole is shifted to the new windward side, and the line that had been the sheet becomes the guy, and conversely the guy becomes the new sheet.

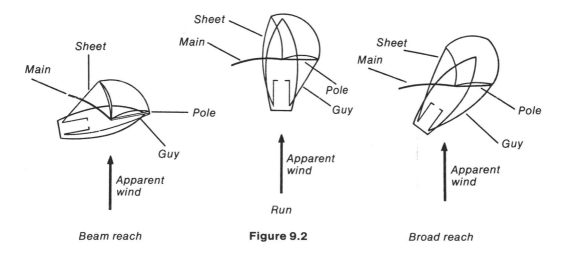

Beam reach   **Figure 9.2**   *Broad reach*

begins to *break*, or curl. then retrim the sheet just until it stops curling. Ease it again, retrim, etc. The rule of trimming a spinnaker sheet is: If the luff is curling, trim it in; if the luff is not curling, ease it out.

The height of the pole is also important to proper spinnaker trim as it controls the height of the tack of the sail relative to the clew, which has a profound effect on performance as well as on the ease of trimming the sail. By adjusting the pole height with the topping lift and downhaul so that the two bottom corners of the sail are horizontal, the sail will take on the symmetrical shape the sailmaker designed it to have. Note: On most boats, you should try to keep the pole close to horizontal, too, by adjusting the inboard end of the pole as necessary along with the topping lift and downhaul. This ensures that the tack of the sail stays as far from the mast as the length of the pole permits, providing the most effective "slot" between the spinnaker and the main.

AVOIDING BROACHES

Since it is possible to capsize or *broach* with a spinnaker up, it is wise not to attempt to fly the sail when it is windy or gusty until you have acquired a reasonable amount of experience and competence sailing under working sails alone.

If you're ready to try the spinnaker, then you already know that different points of sail result in different amounts of heeling force. Specifically, the farther you head downwind toward a very broad reach, the less you heel; the more you head up from that point, the greater the heeling force becomes.

When you're reaching with a spinnaker and get a gust of wind, you heel more. Of course, heeling increases weather helm. So if you don't instantly bear off, this weather helm will cause you to head up more. Heading up more will cause you to heel more, further increasing weather helm. And so on, until the rudder leaves the water and ceases to have the slightest effect on your course, and the ocean pours into your boat. "Terror" does not adequately describe the effect a *spinnaker broach*, as this lamentable chain of events is called, can have on a newcomer to the sport.

To avoid a broach, be alert to gusts and ready to respond immediately by easing your spinnaker sheet and mainsheet and bearing off until the boat is again level and under control. If your mainboom will not go out because it hits the water or the spinnaker sheet, you must ease your boom vang, too. When the gust passes, you can head up and sheet in, but always be ready to ease out and bear off in the next gust.

If a broach does occur, *release your spinnaker sheet. Do not ease the guy*, or the spinnaker will stay full very far away from the boat. *Do not ease the halyard*, or you will ride over the sail and it will wrap itself around your keel—a messy situation. If you ease your spinnaker sheet, mainsheet, and boom vang, the boat will eventually right itself and you can bear off and sheet in. Of course, if you're sailing a centerboard boat and this happens, the boat will not right itself and you've got a bit of work on your hands.

On a dead run in a strong breeze, when the chute is almost entirely to windward, it may tend to pull you over in that direction, resulting in a *windward broach*. This is worse than a leeward broach as it makes a flying jibe likely. To avert a windward broach, head up. The rule for avoiding broaches in hairy conditions is: Steer to keep the boat under the rig.

HOISTING THE SPINNAKER

As with most things, proper preparation is the key to hoisting the chute successfully (getting it up). First, the sail should be *packed* much like a parachute, so that when it does go up it looks like a sail instead of a half hitch. There are numerous techniques for packing a spinnaker with or without a *turtle* (a bag designed for packing a spinnaker), and the best one for any given situation usually depends on the type of boat and the preference of the crew. The idea is to follow at least two of the three edges to make sure there are no twists and end up with a neat package with the head and two clews sticking out in the right places.

It is usually best to launch the chute on the leeward side of the boat in the blanket (wind shadow) of the mainsail, although on larger boats it may be launched off the bow. In any event, secure the turtle (if you use one) so that when the chute goes up, the turtle stays down. Attach the halyard to the head, the guy to the tack, and the sheet to the clew. Watch that the guy is led around outside the windward shrouds and the forestay, and be sure that the halyard, guy, and sheet are all set up to take the sail up through the same "window." If the halyard is rigged to take the sail up between the lower shroud and the mast, and the sheet and guy are rigged to take it up behind the shrouds, you might have to buy a new spinnaker.

Once the lines are attached to the packed sail, set the pole to windward with the guy running through its outboard end. Set it to the height you think is appropriate to the conditions, and be sure both the topping lift and foreguy are cleated.

If you've been doing all this while running downwind, you've probably run out of water by now and have to beat back upwind before hoisting.

To hoist, first make sure you have plenty of room to leeward, get onto a broad reach, and then take a look around for traffic—you're going to be busy for a while. On the skipper's command, raise the halyard and pull the guy simultaneously. Be sure that as the tack of the sail comes around the forestay it makes contact with the outboard end of the pole (shove the pole forward if necessary). Trim the guy until the pole is at a right angle to the wind, then trim the sheet. It's up!

JIBING WITH THE SPINNAKER

Jibing with a spinnaker up is fairly straightforward in theory, but to perform spinnaker jibes well consistently requires a great deal of practice and coordination between the helmsman, foredeck person, and sheet trimmer(s). We will differentiate between a *run-to-run* jibe and a *reach-to-reach* jibe.

A run-to-run jibe works like this: As the helmsman bears off and approaches a run, the foredeck person takes the inboard end of the pole off the mast, walks it over to the leeward side of the boat, and clips it onto the sheet. At this point, the helmsman should jibe the main, steering carefully. The foredeck person then removes the end of the pole from the old guy and clips it onto the mast ring. The person or people trimming the sheets refine the trim of the sail as necessary (Figure 9.3).

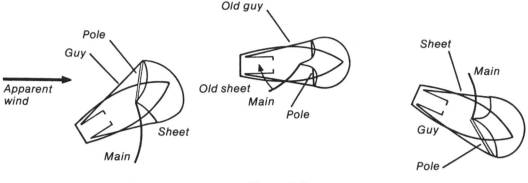

Figure 9.3

On a reach-to-reach jibe (Figure 9.4), it is better to remove the pole from both the mast ring and the old guy as the boat approaches a run and let the helmsman turn the boat through a jibe while the sheet trimmers ease the old sheet and trim the new sheet, essentially keeping the sail downwind as the boat is turned under it. The foredeck person clips the pole onto the new guy as soon as he can reach it, then the other end is clipped onto the mast ring. This requires a lot more practice and coordination than a run-to-run jibe.

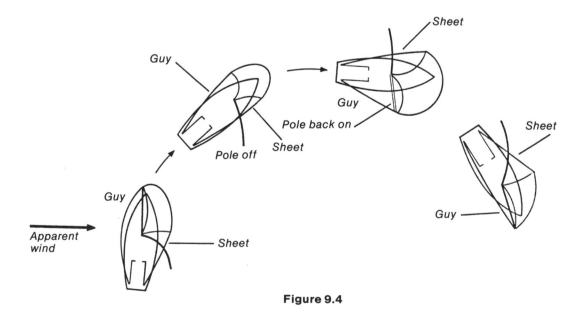

Figure 9.4

DOUSING THE SPINNAKER

While there are several ways of dousing a spinnaker, the easiest is this: On a broad reach or a run, reach under the boom and grab the sheet as close to the clew of the sail as possible. Release the guy and gather the foot of the sail. When you just about have the entire foot in your hands, lower the halyard and bring it into the boat. With this method, the sail comes down in the blanket of the mainsail with almost no force on it. (If you leave the lines attached to the three corners of the sail, it can be hoisted again without the necessity of repacking it, but do check the sail for twists just before the next hoist.) Once the sail is down, take down the pole. You're ready to go back upwind.

Note: So far, the jib has been left out of pictures of boats with spinnakers to avoid confusion. In most cases, however, you can fly a jib in conjunction with a spinnaker with no loss in performance. If you do fly a jib with a spinnaker, however, ease it more than you think you should to ensure smooth air flow over the leeward side of the jib. Otherwise, the turbulence caused by the stalled jib will spoil the flow across the chute, making it more difficult to fly effectively (Figure 9.5).

Figure 9.5

Smooth flow over well-eased jib allows smooth flow over chute.

Turbulence caused by overtrimmed jib does horrible things to chute.

10

HEAVY WEATHER SAILING

The idea of being caught in heavy weather can be frightening until you have experienced enough different kinds of heavy weather conditions to have a good idea of what to expect and some knowledge of how to deal with those conditions.

It is well beyond the scope of this text to attempt to describe all the heavy weather conditions that might be encountered and the wide range of theories for dealing with each of them. There have been many volumes written on the subject, not all of whose authors survived the conditions they researched.

As the above might indicate, the safest way to deal with heavy weather is to avoid it whenever possible; therefore, the prudent sailor *always* obtains an up-to-date marine weather forecast before going out and is prepared to do something else if forecasted conditions are beyond his level of experience.

However, if you sail long enough, you will encounter both storm-like and squall-like conditions. Fortunately, there are sound guidelines for dealing with either of these situations. We will deal with both storm-like and squall-like conditions separately, but by far the most important skill to master in either case is the ability to remain calm. Remaining calm—keeping your wits about you—does not tend to be one's instinctive reaction to severe conditions, but it is essential to survival. It is also a good idea when confronted with any type of heavy weather to don foul-weather gear and life jackets and secure any loose gear in the boat. In addition to increasing your safety, taking these steps helps prepare your state of mind to deal with the conditions. Indeed, when you handle storm- or squall-like conditions correctly (i.e., survive with minimal damage), the experience can be exhilarating.

"Storm-like" refers to conditions where the wind has been blowing and/or building steadily for some time (say, six hours to several days). Such conditions are usually easy to predict and therefore should come as no surprise to anyone who makes a habit of obtaining forecasts before sailing.

The force imparted to your sails by the wind is proportional to the *square* of its velocity. This is not surprising when you consider that if the wind speed triples, for example, then not only do three times as many wind molecules per unit of time encounter your sails, but every one of them is moving three times as fast. A 15-knot breeze is more than twice as forceful as a 10-knot breeze ($15 \times 15 = 225$, $10 \times 10 = 100$), a 20-knot breeze imparts four times the force of a 10-knot breeze, and a 30-knot wind is *nine times* as forceful as a 10-knot breeze!

The velocity of wind that would be severe or dangerous depends on the experience and weight of the crew, the soundness of the boat, how long the wind has been blowing, and the *fetch* in the area where you are sailing. Fetch is the distance the wind blows over water without interruption by land. The greater the fetch, the larger and more severe the waves. Also, the longer the wind has been blowing, the larger and more severe the waves (Figure 10.1).

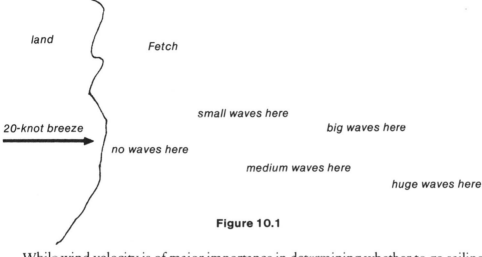

Figure 10.1

While wind velocity is of major importance in determining whether to go sailing and how much sail to keep up if you do, large waves wreak more havoc than strong wind does. In relatively open water, 20 knots of wind could easily create 6- to 10-foot waves. In an open boat, these would be extreme conditions. The same wind speed in protected water with one- or two-foot waves, for example, could provide fine sailing.

What happens as a boat sails upwind in waves is this: As the boat slides down a wave, it accelerates, then crashes into the trough, suddenly decelerating. Depending on how badly the boat crashes into the trough, a tremendous strain can be put on the rig as it attempts to keep going while the boat attempts to stop. Ocean-racing boats with no sails up have actually broken their masts as a result of the sudden shock load of falling off steep waves.

If it is not too windy to sail upwind, the solution is to concentrate on steering as smooth a course as possible through the waves. Generally, this means heading up slightly as you go up the face of a wave (as the boat slows and the apparent wind shifts *aft*) and falling off somewhat as you accelerate down the back of the wave (as the apparent wind shifts forward). In order to maintain steering control, do not attempt to point high under such conditions; foot off to keep up your speed.

Sailing downwind in large waves can present an assortment of difficulties, depending on the size and shape of the waves compared to the length of the boat. If the waves are large enough, expect the following: As a wave approaches, it lifts the stern. If the boat is aligned in anything other than a stern-to-the-wave configuration, the wave will also cause the boat to heel. As you remember from the section on balance, a boat tends to turn opposite the direction in which it heels (i.e., if the boat heels to leeward, it tends to head up; if it heels to windward, it tends to fall off), so as the boat heels, it immediately tends to turn more beam to the wave. In this position, the only part of the boat in the water on the down side of the wave is the keel, and the boat may "trip" over the keel, resulting in a *knockdown*, or broach. After a few knockdowns, you learn to steer with intense concentration in order to keep the stern aligned with the waves and the boat upright (Figure 10.2).

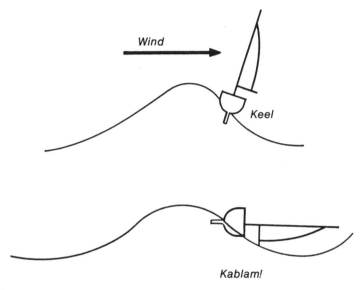

Wind

Keel

Kablam!

Figure 10.2

A boat sailing downwind in extreme wave conditions may be in for a knockdown. *The wave heels the boat, the boat heads up and ends up beam to the wave. In this configuration you can see how the forces of the wind and the wave will essentially trip the boat over its keel, resulting in the knockdown. A seaworthy keel boat will generally recover from even a severe knockdown without much damage; however, you would not want to be in an open boat under such extreme conditions.*

A critical component of successful sailing in storm-like conditions, whether upwind or downwind, is continuous monitoring of your sail combination and sail trim to maintain exactly the right amount of power for the conditions. Too much power results in continuous knockdowns, weather helm, sail and/or rig destruction, and other unpleasantness. Too little, and you move too slowly to steer.

As wind velocity increases from civilized toward storm-like conditions, your first step should be to follow procedures outlined in the section on sail-shape control to flatten your sails, reduce power, and maintain balance. As the wind continues to build, douse your genoa and hoist a jib. If you continue to be overpowered, reef your main. If you can double reef, that would be the next step. If you are overpowered with a small jib and a double-reefed main, it is time to take down one of your sails. A boat with a deep bow will sail pretty well on jib alone on any point of sail; a boat with a shallow bow will sail better on reefed or double-reefed main alone. However, in large waves, do not sail on jib alone (unless it is a tiny "storm jib") because the tremendous shock load caused by waves would be transmitted to the mast at a single point—the point where the jib halyard enters the mast. This has broken many a mast. The luff of even a double- or triple-reefed main, on the other hand, helps support the mast.

Obviously, sailing in extreme conditions of wind and waves is not for beginners. The important thing, however, is to know what conditions are safe (those in which you can sail under complete control without frequent luffing of sails), given the experience of you and your crew. As your skill increases, try sailing on progressively windier days, but do not exceed your limits. In my experience, beginning sailors fresh out of a good instruction program can handle 10-to-15-knot winds safely; experienced racing crews can handle 30 knots safely if wave conditions are not too outrageous. Experienced, sane individuals do not go out in small open boats in conditions much more extreme than this.

A squall, unlike a storm, is of short duration (generally five to 30 minutes) and does not last long enough to create serious waves. It can, however, generate wind blasts of 30 to 50 knots, possibly more. Generally, the first blasts of a squall are the most severe; if you survive these, you will probably make it through the squall. Unfortunately, a 50-knot gust will knock down any boat with sails up, and while you are not likely to sail an open boat at sea where storm conditions might cause a dangerous knockdown, a squall can occur anywhere.

A squall occurs in conjunction with an approaching cold front (in the northern hemisphere they generally approach from the northwest). The greater the temperature gradient, the more severe the squall. As the heavier air of the cold mass wedges its way in under the warmer air, the warm air is forced up, in some cases as high as 50,000 or 60,000 feet. There it contracts and cools, forms clouds and rain, and, being colder and therefore heavier than the air now below it, begins to fall, accelerating. By the time the rain and wind reach the surface, they may be traveling as fast as 50 knots.

Individual squalls, while capable of causing a great deal of damage, tend to be local and are extremely difficult to forecast accurately. A forecast may indicate a *possibility of squalls*, but then again, it may not.

Fortunately, the alert sailor watching the sky to the northwest does receive some advance notice of an approaching squall. As a squall forms and the impinging cold air mass forces the warmer air to rise, cool, and condense, you can see rapidly forming, vertically developed clouds to the northwest. As these clouds darken and become more ominous, a squall becomes more and more imminent. When all this is occuring to the northwest, you are in for a squall.

When you first notice the signs of squall activity in the northwest (and you should always be alert to this possibility, particularly on summer evenings), take action. If you can get back to your mooring before the squall strikes, that's best. If you can anchor in the lee of a land mass where you will be protected from fierce northwesterly winds, that's good, too. Take any steps necessary to avoid being immediately to windward of land (i.e., land to your southeast) when the first blasts of the squall strike. In any case, *well before the first blast of the squall hits, get your mainsail down and secured.* If you have not made it to a mooring or anchorage, be ready to drop and secure your jib and run downwind under bare poles (if the gusts are severe) until the squall passes. A severe squall can knock down a keel boat on jib alone if the boat is not sailing on a run when it hits.

If you have gotten your mainsail down before the first gust of the squall and left yourself room to leeward, you will most likely survive the squall with no more than a soaking and a rush of excitement, and after a few minutes you will be able to raise sail again and continue on.

11

SEAMANSHIP

eamanship is the art of staying out of trouble. Continuous navigation is only a part of good seamanship.

As with most things, seamanship cannot be learned simply by reading about it. It must be learned through experience. However, there are a few points that, if kept in mind, will facilitate this learning process and enhance your safety:

1. Do not exceed your level of competence. Sailing in wind or wave conditions too heavy for your experience can lead to embarrassment, serious injury, even death. Accidental jibes, collisions resulting from lack of boat-handling experience in heavy air, etc., can spoil your day. Stick to conditions you know you can handle, and gradually work up to stronger conditions as you gain experience.
2. In marginal conditions, stay in waters that you know. When your hands are full just handling the boat, it is not good seamanship to get yourself into a situation requiring fancy navigation too!
3. Stay vigilant. It is dangerously easy to forget to look out for other boat traffic, but you must do this at all times while sailing.
4. Navigate continuously!
5. Always check the weather report before sailing. If the forecast calls for storms or squalls, play your favorite heavy weather sport instead.
6. Make use of Murphy's Law: "If something can go wrong, it will." The law has literally thousands of corollaries, including: "If it can go wrong at various times, it will go wrong at the worst possible time"; "If it can go wrong in a number of different ways, it will go wrong in the worst possible way"; "If a halyard is going to jam, it will do so only when you need to get your sail down *immediately*"; etc.

Murphy's Law turns out to be a useful principle of seamanship. In any given situation, it prompts the questions: "What can go wrong here?"; "In how many different ways?"; and most important, "How are we prepared to deal with those possibilities?"

Some examples of Murphy's Law in action:

M.L. #727: Sometimes, particularly when it is quite windy, masts fall down. When they do, they usually fall to leeward. Accordingly, under extreme conditions, experienced sailors try to avoid placing themselves where the rig would land if it did fall. For similar reasons, experienced sailors avoid lining up important parts of their anatomy with rope or wire under a great deal of tension.

M.L. #686: When a sail must come down fast without a snag, the halyard will jam. So when you're approaching a dock downwind under jib only, and you need to drop your jib and coast the last 10 boat lengths, the experienced sailor will neatly recoil the halyard, uncleat it, and begin to lower the sail early enough so he could still turn the boat and bail out in case the halyard jams anyway.

M.L. #13270: When you finally sight that buoy you've been expecting, heave a sigh of relief, and put away your chart, chances are good it's not the buoy you think it is. The experienced navigator, upon sighting a navigational aid, carefully scans the entire appropriate area of the chart to see if there are any other aids that it could be.

Murphy's Law has numerous applications, and I find it a useful way of anticipating problems.

If you sail long enough, you will probably have to deal with an assortment of vicissitudes. For example, I know of no experienced sailors who have never run aground or had someone fall overboard while sailing. Use your imagination; almost anything can occur, and in accord with Murphy's Law, we should be ready for it.

SAFETY PRECAUTIONS

Accordingly, there are some basic safety precautions one must take while sailing:

1. Always have at least one life jacket (or "Personal Flotation Device," as they are officially known) for each person on board, and if conditions are rough, wear them. Weak swimmers and small children should *always* wear a life jacket while sailing. All PFDs should be in working order, and you should have sizes appropriate for your crew. If you are not wearing them, stow them where you can get to them easily (i.e., not under all the other gear in the cockpit locker). At least one PFD or a throwable lifering or horseshoe buoy should be immediately available at all times in the event someone falls overboard.

In addition to the real possibility of saving someone's life, this advice in regard to PFDs represents a legal requirement that the Coast Guard, appropriately enough, takes rather seriously.

Other legal requirements motivated by safety considerations include the carrying of a horn or whistle and day and night visual distress signals (flares). Boats with auxiliary engines are required to carry approved fire extinguishers. Boats over 26 feet in length must carry a throwable PFD in addition to the required one per person, and boats over 39 feet are also required to have a bell for use when anchored in fog.

2. In addition to the above legal requirements, the following must be considered a minimum list of essential safety gear under most sailing conditions: chart, compass, paddle, pump, and anchor and rode. A first-aid kit, some basic tools, and extra clothing are worth bringing too. Perversely enough, boats occasionally run aground, the wind often dies in the evening, and auxiliary engines sometimes fail, any of which could result in your being out longer than you originally expected.

Publications such as Chapman's *Piloting Seamanship and Small Boat Handling* contain more comprehensive information on legal requirements and recommended safety equipment for vessels of different descriptions.

MAN-OVERBOARD PROCEDURES

Anyone in command of a sailboat should know—and be proficient at—man-overboard procedures. Ideally, someone else on board should be proficient at them too, in case the person in command falls overboard. The difference between responding correctly in a man-overboard situation and responding incorrectly can be tragically significant.

When a person falls overboard from a moving boat, your immediate reaction should be to throw the person a life jacket or other flotation device.

The next step is to assign a crew member to observe and constantly point to the victim. It is remarkably difficult to see a person floating in the water if you don't know exactly where he is.

Next, alert your entire crew to the emergency so everyone is available to assist.

You must now expeditiously bring the boat to a stop alongside the victim and pick him up. This is similar to landing at a mooring, in that the boat must be pointed approximately into the wind on its final approach in order to be brought to a complete stop. There are a couple of important differences, however. First, it's no big deal to run over a mooring buoy, but a person is another matter. Second, when mooring you want to stop with the bow of the boat exactly at the buoy; when rescuing a man overboard you want to stop with the victim alongside the boat so you can pull him out of the water. Of the two basic techniques offered in the section on mooring, the second one is better for rescuing an overboard victim—i.e., approach not quite head-to-wind but close-hauled, luffing or sheeting in your sails as necessary to control speed and steering (Figure 11.1).

In addition to facilitating more precise boat-speed control, making your final approach on a close-hauled course enables you to stop the boat with the victim to windward, which makes it easier to see him clearly, since the sails will be out of the way to leeward, and easier to get him back into the boat with sails, boom, and associated rigging out of the way to leeward. Also, it is much better to have the victim driven toward the boat by wind and waves than the boat driven onto the victim.

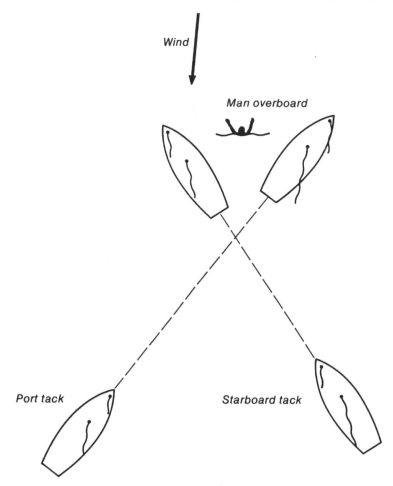

Figure 11.1   Final Approach Toward Victim

Further, if you are sailing a centerboard boat, it will capsize if you attempt to pull a person out of the water on the leeward side.

Notice that the most direct route to either the port- or starboard-tack close-hauled approach depends on where you are when you're ready to begin to turn and retrieve the victim. If you are above the final approach course, fall off and jibe. If you're below the final approach course, head up and tack (Figure 11.2). When you stop alongside a man overboard, have a paddle or a boat hook ready for him to grab or to grab him with if necessary.

Recognizing the quickest route to a close-hauled approach course immediately after someone falls in and executing the entire retrieval without flaw cannot be learned without doing it over and over again. I strongly recommend practicing man-overboard drills (using a life jacket as the victim, preferably) until you are confident that you could do it correctly even under the pressure of someone actually falling off your boat.

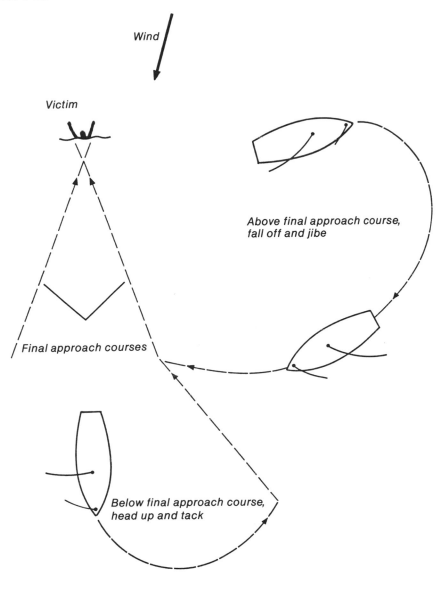

Wind

Victim

Above final approach course, fall off and jibe

Final approach courses

Below final approach course, head up and tack

Figure 11.2

Seamanship means being prepared for whatever is likely to occur. Yet one of the difficulties associated with a chapter on safety and seamanship is that unlike the rest of the material in this book, which applies often, this information becomes meaningful only when trouble occurs. It is fine to learn to tack in headers long after you encounter your first header, but it is too late to teach your crew the proper way to put on life jackets after your boat sinks! While seamanship cannot be acquired without experience, the prudent sailor constantly seeks to improve his expertise in this area. This is probably the most important concept in this book.

GLOSSARY

Aback: With the wind on the wrong side of the sails.

Abaft: Behind an object in relation to the bow, i.e., "abaft the mast" means "behind the mast."

Abeam: At a right angle to the line of the keel, off the beam.

Aft: Toward the stern.

Alee: Downwind, to the leeward side.

Amidships (also *midships*): The center of the vessel. May refer to either the fore-and-aft or athwartship direction.

Apparent wind: The wind direction that is felt on the deck of a moving vessel. It differs from the true wind as a result of the vessel's speed and course.

Anchor light (also *riding light*): A white light carried high in the vessel, often at the masthead, and visible in a 360-degree circle.

Astern: Abaft the vessel.

Auxiliary: A vessel propelled by both sails and engine, separately or together. Also, the engine in an auxiliary.

Back: The wind backs when it changes direction to the left. See *veer*.

Backstay: The part of the standing rigging that supports the mast from the aft part of the vessel. May be "permanent" or "running," depending upon whether the backstay is fixed or adjustable.

Ballast: Weight, usually iron, lead, or other heavy substance, carried low in the vessel to increase stability.

Bare poles: With no sail set, as in a storm.

Battens: Light wood or plastic strips fitted to support the roach of a sail.

Batten pockets: Pockets sewn into the aft end of a sail to hold the battens.

Beam: A timber fitted athwartship to support the deck. Also, the maximum breadth of a vessel.

Beat: Sailing to windward on alternate tacks.

Bermudan rig: A triangular sail with the luff secured to the mast. Also called *marconi rig*. Original name, now rarely used, was *leg-o-mutton* rig.

Bilge: The turn of the hull between the topside and the bottom. Also, the dark, smelly place above the keel where all the oily water collects.

Boom: The spar to which the foot of a fore-and-aft sail is fastened, e.g., *mainboom, stays'l boom*.

Bow: The forward end of the vessel. Also called the *pointy end*.

Bowsprit: A spar extending forward of the bow from which the headsails (jibs) are set. *Bowsprit shrouds* or *whisker shrouds* support the bowsprit athwartship.

Bulkhead: A vertical partition, either athwartship or fore-and-aft, that forms the "walls" of the various compartments. In modern yachts, most bulkheads add structural strength as well.

By-the-head: Used to describe a vessel that is trimmed down forward below her designed waterline.

By-the-lee: Sailing downwind with the wind and the mainboom on the same side of the vessel. Can be dangerous.

By-the-stern: Used to describe a vessel that is trimmed down aft below her designed waterline.

Catboat: Single-masted sailboat, carrying mainsail only, no headsails.

CB (Center of Buoyancy): The center of the vessel's displacement.

CE (Center of Effort): The center of the vessel's sail area.

CF (Center of Flotation): The center of the vessel's waterline area.

CLP (Center of Lateral Pressure, also CLR, the Center of Lateral Resistance): The center of the underwater area of the vessel viewed in profile.

CG: The Center of Gravity. Also, *VCG*, the vertical center of gravity. Note that the fore-and-aft CG must be at the same location as the CB.

Centerboard: A device that can be lowered through the hull to increase the lateral area in order to reduce leeway under sail.

Chainplates: The fittings on a yacht that accept the lower ends of the shrouds in order to support the mast.

Clew: The lower aft corner of a fore-and-aft sail; the two lower corners of a square sail.

Close-hauled: Sailing to windward with sails trimmed as close to midships as possible.

Close-winded: A boat that will sail well to windward. *Weatherly* is another term used to denote this desirable feature.

Come about: To change tacks by bringing the bow through the eye of the wind.

Cutter: A single-masted yacht with two or more headsails, the mast being located farther aft than the mast in a sloop.

Daggerboard: A centerboard that is hoisted vertically in its trunk instead of pivoting.

Dead light: Fixed glass ports. Also, the metal plate that closes off an opening portlight in an emergency.

Deck: The planked "floor" of a vessel. Note that in yachts the interior deck is called the *cabin sole*; the decks are exterior.

Displacement: The weight of water displaced by the vessel; the weight of the vessel.

Double-ender: A sharp sterned hull.

Downhaul: A line or tackle used to pull down a sail or spar *(spinnaker pole downhaul, jib downhaul)*.

Draft: The depth of water required to float a vessel. Also refers to the shape of a sail.

Drag: Used to denote resistance. Also, a fin or keel that increases its draft toward the aft end is said to have drag to its shape.

Drop keel: Old term for *centerboard*.

Eddy: Water or air currents moving in confused, circular patterns.

Fair: Used to describe a hull without distortions, humps, bumps, or hollows.

Fairlead: An eye of plastic or wood used to lead lines in the desired direction.

Fiberglass: Actually should be called *fiberglass reinforced plastic* (FRP). See text.

Fin keel: A deep, narrow fin, separate from the rudder, to provide lateral resistance. It is not actually a keel.

Foot: The lower edge of a sail. Also, to perform; i.e., to *outfoot* means to sail faster than a rival.

Fore-and-aft: Along the line of the keel; i.e., in a fore-and-aft rig, the sails are set in the direction of the keel rather than athwartships.

Foremast: The forward mast of a schooner.

Foresail: The sail set on the foremast of a schooner.

Forefoot: Where the keel meets the stem.

Freeboard: The distance from the water to the deck at side, or sheerline.

Full-and-by: Sailing as close to the wind as possible with all sails drawing.

Gaff rig: A rig in which the mainsail is quadrilateral and its upper side, or head, is fastened to a gaff spar attached to the mast.

Gale: A storm with wind speed of 34 to 40 knots.

Galley: The cooking compartment. Also, a type of rowing craft.

Genoa: A large jib that overlaps the mast and is sheeted well aft. Also called *jenny*.

Go about: To change tack by bringing the bow through the eye of the wind. See *come about*.

Gooseneck: The metal fitting that secures the boom to the mast.

Goosewing jibe: A bad jibe resulting in the boom and gaff ending up on opposite sides of the mast.

Ground tackle: The anchor, chain, rode, etc.

Gunkholing: Cruising in shallow water and overnighting in small, quiet coves.

Gybe: Changing tack by passing the wind over the stern rather than the bow. *Jibe* is the more common spelling.

Halyards (also *halliards*): Lines used to hoist sails.

Hanks: Fittings sewn onto the headsails for fastenings the sails to the stays.

Hard-a-lee: The command to put the helm over to come about.

Hard over: To put the helm over as far as possible in either direction.

Hauling part: That part of a tackle that is pulled upon, the other end being the *standing part.*

Head: The marine toilet, also the toilet compartment. Also, the upper part of a gaff sail or the upper corner of a jibheaded sail.

Headboard: A wood or metal fitting sewn into the head of a Bermudan sail.

Headstay: The stay running from the masthead to the stemhead or the bowsprit end, if fitted.

Heave-to: To bring the boat's head to wind so that she will stay there. This is done by putting the vessel on the wind with helm down and sails trimmed flat so that she will alternately come up and then fall off a bit. The purpose is to hold the general position when riding out a gale.

Heel: The lower part of the mast or rudder. Also, the athwartship inclination of a vessel.

Helm: The tiller or steering wheel.

Helm's-alee: A warning sounded by the helmsman when tacking to brace the crew to their duties.

Hiking: To get the crew weight to windward outside the rail for added stability.

Inboard: Towards the centerline of the vessel.

Initial stability: The stability of the vessel at small angles of heel.

Jib: A triangular sail set forward of the fore or mainmast.

Jibheaded: An older term for the *Bermudan, marconi,* or *leg-o'-mutton* mainsail.

Jibe: See *gybe.*

Jibheaded rig: See *Bermudan rig, marconi rig.*

Jiffy reef: A form of slab reefing with reef tackles arranged so that reefing can be done quickly and simply.

Jumpers: Stays set up to support the masthead of a ¾ or ⅞ rig. *Jumper struts* are the spreaders fitted to hold these stays in position and apply their force to the mast.

Jury rig: An emergency rig set up when dismasted. Any gear rigged to carry out the job of a broken part.

Keel: The backbone of a vessel to which the floors and frames are fastened. The term *fin keel* is really a poor one; it should be simply *fin* as the structure does not truly serve the purpose of a keel.

Ketch: See text. A two-masted vessel in which the mizzen is forward of the rudderpost and/or over 15 percent of the total sail area.

Knot: One nautical mile per hour. A *nautical mile* equals 1.151 land miles, or 6,076 feet.

Lateen: A triangular sail set from a yard along the luff of the sail.

Lay-to: See *heave-to.*

Leach (also *leech*): The after side of a fore-and-aft sail; the edges of a square sail.

Lead: The distance that the center of sail area is ahead of the center of lateral resistance. See text.

Lee: Downwind, away from the wind.

Lee helm: Having to hold the helm to the lee side in order to maintain a course. Undesirable. See text, *helm balance.*

Lee side: The side away from the wind.

Leeward: Downwind. One vessel is said to be to leeward of another.

Leeway: The movement of a vessel to leeward due to the force of the wind on the sails.

Load waterline: The waterline at which the designer prays the boat will float.

Loose footed: A fore-and-aft sail not attached to a boom or club.

Luff: The leading edge of a fore-and-aft sail. Also, to luff a sail is to allow the vessel to come head-to-wind, or to ease the sheets, so that the wind pressure on the leading edge of the sail is relieved.

Mainmast: The forward mast in yawls and ketches; the aft mast in a schooner.

Mainsail: The sail set abaft the mast on sloops and cutters and from the mainmast of ketches, yawls, and schooners.

Marconi rig: See *Bermudan rig.*

Mast step: The structural member that supports the heel of the mast.

Midships: The fore-and-aft center of the vessel.

Mizzenmast: The after mast of a yawl or ketch. See *jigger.*

Mizzensail (usually just *mizzen*): The sail set abaft the mizzenmast.

Mizzen staysail: A triangular sail set flying from the mizzenmast head, tacked to the deck forward to windward, and sheeted to the mizzenboom. Used when reaching and running. It is badly named as it is not set on a stay and so is not truly a staysail.

Near gale: Storm with wind speeds of 28 to 33 knots.

No higher: An order meaning to sail no closer to the wind.

North river jibe: Jibing quickly without first hauling in the mainsheet. Can be dangerous.

Off-the-wind: To sail downwind.

Offing: Well out to sea but with land in sight.

On the beam: At a right angle to the line of the keel.

On the bow: 45 degrees or less from the bow.

On the quarter: 45 degrees or less from the stern.

On the wind: Close-hauled.

Outpoint: To sail closer to the wind than a rival yacht.

Out of trim: To be down by the bow or stern, or with an athwartship list.

Outboard: Outside of the hull of the vessel. Also, a portable motor.

Outfoot: To sail faster than a rival yacht.

Outhaul: A fitting or line used to haul out the clew of a sail.

Outsail: To make better speed and/or point higher than a rival yacht.

Overboard: Over the side; in the water.

Overhang: The projection of the bow and/or stern beyond the ends of the waterline.

Painter: The towing line made fast to the bow of a dinghy.

Part: One section of a rope or tackle. Also, to break.

Pawls: The device in a winch or windlass that prevents it from turning backward.

Pay off: To turn the bow away from the wind.

Peak: The upper aft corner of a gaff sail. Also, the end of the gaff. Also, a compartment in the ends of the vessel; see *forepeak*.

Peak halyard: The line that hoists the peak of the gaff.

Pinch: To point slightly too high to windward, slowing the vessel and causing the sails to luff.

Pitch: The falling and rising of a vessel in a fore-and-aft direction. Also, the distance the propeller would move forward in one revolution if it were threading into a solid material. Also, a material used to pay the seams of a vessel.

Pitch pole: A disaster in which a breaking sea causes a vessel to cartwheel her stern over her bow.

Plain sail: The working sails.

Plow: Another name for the patented *CQR* (secure) anchor.

Poop: The raised after deck at the stern of a vessel.

Pooped: Having a sea break over the stern.

Port: The left side of the vessel when looking forward. Old term for port was *larboard*. Also, an opening in the side of a vessel, i.e., *gun port, portlight* (window).

Port tack: Sailing with the wind coming over the port side.

Preventer: A line running from the boom forward to prevent an accidental jibe.

Pulpit: The railing at the bow or stern.

Quarter: The side of the vessel abaft the beam and forward of the stern, the aft "corner," in effect.

Rake: The angle of the masts or deck structures.

Reach: To sail on a course between close-hauled and running free. *Close reach*—wind forward of the beam. *Beam reach*—wind abeam. *Broad reach*—wind on the quarter.

Ready about: The order given to prepare to tack the vessel.

Reef: To reduce sail area. *Close-reefed*—the sail is reduced to its last set of reef points.

Reef cringle: A grommet or eye in the leach and tack of the sail at the ends of the reef.

Reef earing: The line attaching the reef cringle to the boom (*luff earing, leach earing*).

Reef points: Short pieces of rope set in the sail at intervals to secure the foot of the sail when reefed.

Reef tackle: The line that pulls the reef down to the boom until the earings can be tied off. In modern reefing the tackles may be permanent and separate earings not used.

Riding light: Anchor light.

Rig: A vessel's arrangement of masts and sails. Also, to set up the masts and rigging in a vessel.

Rigging: The wires and ropes that support the masts (*standing rigging*) and hoist and trim the spars and sails (*running rigging*).

Right: To return to upright, as to right a capsized dinghy.

Roach: The curve in the leach of a sail. In the foot of a genoa it is called *foot roach.*

Rode: The anchor line. Often *anchor rode.*

Roll: Side-to-side oscillation of a vessel.

Roller furling gear: The sail rolls up on a wire luff or aluminum foil. Commonly used for headsails, becoming more frequent on mainsails either inside or just abaft the mast. Roller furled sails cannot have roach or battens.

Roller reefing gear: A method of reefing by rolling the sail around the boom. Now obsolete, largely replaced by slab or jiffy reefing.

Rudder: The plate at the stern used to steer a vessel.

Run: The hull of the vessel underwater toward the stern. Also, to sail downwind, as in "running free."

Running backstays (also *runners*)**:** Temporary backstays that are set up to tension the jib or staysail luff. The weather backstay is set up when changing tack, and the leeward backstay is let go.

Running lights: Lights carried when underway at night.

Schooner: A fore-and-aft rigged vessel with two to seven masts. The usual two-masted schooner has a foremast and a taller mainmast abaft the foremast.

Scow: A shoal-draft, square ended vessel. The *scow sloop* is a popular open racing class in the Midwest.

Screw: Another term for *propeller.*

Scud: To run before a gale with storm sails or no sails. Also, driving mist or broken clouds moving fast under nimbus clouds.

Scuppers: Drains on deck or in the cockpit to carry water overboard.

Seacock: A type of valve connecting a vessel's piping to the seawater.

Seakindly: A vessel with an easy motion in heavy seas.

Seawater: Weighs 64 pounds per cubic foot. Thirty-five cubic feet weigh one ton, or 2,240 pounds.

Seaworthy: A vessel that is well designed, built, equipped, and in satisfactory condition to meet conditions at sea.

Seize: Binding ropes together with light line or marline.

Set: The direction of the current; the direction in which a vessel is moved by the tide and/or wind.

Shackle: A horseshoe-shaped metal fitting with a bolt or pin across the open end.

Sharpie: A flat bottom, shoal-draft hull developed in the Long Island Sound area. See text.

Sheer: The curve of the deck line.

Sheet: The line attached to the clew of a sail, or to the boom of a boomed sail, in order to trim the sail.

Shoot: To luff and move to windward by the vessel's momentum.

Short board: A short tack.

Shorten sail: To reduce sail area by reefing or taking down a sail.

Shrouds: The wires that support the mast athwartships. See *stays.*

Side lights: The red (port) and green (starboard) running lights.

Skeg: The extension of the hull forward of and supporting the rudder.

Slab reefing: Reefing by lowering the sail to a line of reef points sewn in parallel to the foot.

Sloop: A single-masted vessel with one or more headsails. The mast is farther forward than in a cutter, though the distinction is a narrow one today.

Slot effect: The theory that the improvement in speed from carrying a large overlapping jib is due to the effect of accelerated air flow to the lee side of the mainsail, rather than simply to the larger sail area of the jib.

Snatch block: A block that can open to allow the line to be placed in it, rather than having to pull the whole length through the block.

Sole: The cabin floor.

Spade rudder: A rudder that is supported only by the strength of its rudder stock and is not attached to the hull or to a skeg.

Spars: A general term for the mast, boom, gaff, spinnaker pole, etc.

Spinnaker: A large, light triangular headsail used off the wind and when reaching. Sets with its tack held outboard by a spinnaker pole. A very unseamanlike sail, in my view.

Spreaders: The wood or metal (aluminum) struts used to spread the shrouds to a better staying angle.

Squatting: The sinking of the stern due to excess speed.

Stability: The moment or force that tends to return a vessel to upright. See text.

Stanchions: Upright support posts. The term is usually used to mean the lifeline stanchions.

Standing backstay: One that is permanently set up and not shifted with the tack. Also called *permanent backstay.*

Standing part: The part of a rope or tackle that is made fast to an eye or block.

Standing rigging: The rigging that supports the mast, consisting of stays and shrouds.

Starboard: The right side of the vessel when looking forward.

Starboard tack: Sailing with the wind coming over the starboard side.

Start: To ease off on a line.

Stay: The wire rigging that supports the mast from forward. The backstay supports it from aft.

Staysail: The triangular sail set on the forestay.

Staysail schooner: A schooner in which the foresail is replaced by a staysail set from the mainmast.

Stem: The timber or steel bar that supports the planking between the keel and the deck. On a fiberglass boat, that part of the hull at the bow between the waterline and the deck.

Step: see *mast step.* To step a mast is to set it in the vessel.

Stern: The after part of a vessel.

Storm: Officially, wind speeds of 48 to 55 knots.

Storm sails: Sails of small size and heavy material, usually hand roped on the edges for extra strength, intended for gale winds. Commonly, a storm jib and storm trysail are carried.

Strong gale: A storm with wind speeds of 41 to 47 knots.

Swaging: A terminal fused to the end of wire rigging; the act of fitting such a terminal.

Swamped: A boat awash with water.

Tack: A course sailed with the wind on one side of the yacht. To *tack* or to *change tack* is to change course (*come about*) by bringing the wind across the bow to the other tack. Also, the forward lower corner of a sail.

Tackle (pronounced *taykle*): A purchase composed of rope and blocks to increase power. The power is equal to the total number of running parts, less a small amount for friction.

Tangs: Metal fittings that attach the rigging to the mast.

Telltale: A light yarn or ribbon suspended in the rigging to indicate wind direction.

Tensile strength: The measure of a material to withstand a pulling strain, measured in tons or thousands of pounds per square inch.

Throat: That part of the gaff nearest the mast. The forward upper corner of a gaff sail or spritsail.

Tiller: A wood or metal bar connected to the rudderpost to steer a vessel.

Toe rail: A low rail around the deck edge.

Topmast: The mast next above the lower mast.

Topping lift: A line running from the mast to the boom to support the boom when the sail is lowered. A *spinnaker-pole topping lift* supports the spinnaker pole.

Topsail schooner: A schooner having a square topsail on the foremast.

Topsides: The area of the hull between the boot top and the deck.

Transom: The stern of a square sterned vessel.

Traveler: The track with car or slide, or the athwartship rod, to which a boom is sheeted. A *bridle* is a wire traveler.

Trim: The fore-and-aft flotation of a vessel. "Trimmed by the head" means trimmed down by the bow.

Turnbuckle: A metal fitting composed of two bolts threaded into a central cylinder. The bolts have eyes or jaws at the ends to fit onto the rigging and chainplates. The turnbuckle can be adjusted to tension the rigging as required.

Underfoot: The anchor is on the bottom, and the anchor line is straight up and down.

Underway: A vessel that is cast off from the pier and has her anchor up (whether she is moving or not).

Vangs: Lines leading from the peak of the gaff to the deck to trim the gaff amidship. *Boom vang*—a tackle to haul down on the boom to flatten the mainsail.

Veer: To pay out anchor line. Also, for the wind to change direction to the right.

Vessel: A general term for any floating structure.

Wake: The disturbed water behind a moving vessel.

Waterline: The line at which a vessel floats. Lines used by a naval architect in fairing up the drawing of a hull.

Weather: Toward the wind. The side of the vessel toward the wind is the weather side, also the *windward side*.

Weather helm: The tendency of a vessel to come head-to-wind, requiring that the helm be to weather to maintain the desired course.

Weatherly: A vessel that performs well to windward.

Weigh: Raise the anchor.

Wheel: The steering wheel. Also, a term for *propeller*.

Whisker pole: A pole used to hold out the clew of a headsail when running.

Wide berth: A safe and comfortable distance from another vessel, a shoal, or the land.

Winch: A mechanical device for increasing power for hauling on running rigging.

Windward: The direction from which the wind is blowing. See *weather*.

Wing-and-wing: To sail downwind with sails on opposite sides of the vessel. Also called *wung out*.

Working sails: Those sails that are regularly used, excluding light sails and storm sails.

Working to windward *or* **Work up:** To tack to windward.

Yacht: A vessel used for pleasure. A hole in the water into which the owner pours money.

Yaw: To steer badly, veer continually off course, particularly when running.

Yawl: A two-masted vessel in which the mizzenmast is set abaft the sternpost or the mizzensail is less than 15 percent of the total sail area.

Zincs: Zinc plates fitted to the hull to prevent electrolysis.

Zulu: A Scottish lug rigged fishing boat of double-ended hull form.

BIBLIOGRAPHY

Brewer, Ted. *Ted Brewer Explains Yacht Design*. Camden, ME: International Marine Publishing Company, 1985.

Coles, Adlard K., *Heavy Weather Sailing, 3rd Edition*. Clinton Corners, NY: John de Graff, 1981.

Gibbs, Tony. *The Coastal Navigator's Notebook*. Camden, ME: International Marine Publishing Company, 1979.

Henderson, Richard. *Sea Sense, 2nd Edition*. Camden, ME: International Marine Publishing Company, 1979.

Henderson, Richard. *Understanding Rigs and Rigging*. Camden, ME: International Marine Publishing Company, 1985.

Maloney, Elbert S. *Piloting Seamanship and Small Boat Handling, 56th Edition*. New York, NY: Hearst, 1983.

Marchaj, C.A. *Sailing Theory and Practice—Revised Edition*. New York, NY: Dodd, Mead & Company, 1982.

Meisel, Tony. *Undersail*. New York, NY: Macmillan, 1982.

Ross, Wallace. *Sail Power—Revised Edition*. New York, NY: Knopf, 1984.

Rousmaniere, John. *The Annapolis Book of Seamanship*. New York, NY: Simon and Schuster, 1983.

Schlereth, Hewitt. *Commonsense Coastal Navigation*. New York, NY: W.W. Norton and Company, 1982.

Sherwood, Richard M. *A Field Guide to Sailboats*. Boston, MA: Houghton Mifflin Company, 1984.

Sleightholme, Des. *Better Boat Handling*. Newport, RI: Seven Seas Press, 1983.

Tate, William H. *Mariners Guide to the Rules of the Road, 2nd Edition*. Annapolis, MD: Naval Institute Press, 1982.

Toss, Brion. *The Rigger's Apprentice*. Camden, ME: International Marine Publishing Company, 1984.

INDEX